The Bounce Bible

2nd Edition

Ivan 'Doc' Holiday

Outskirts Press, Inc.
Denver, Colorado

The opinions expressed in this manuscript are solely the opinions of the author and do not represent the opinions or thoughts of the publisher. The author has represented and warranted full ownership and/or legal right to publish all the materials in this book.

The Bouncer's Bible
2nd Edition
All Rights Reserved.
Copyright © 2011 Ivan 'Doc' Holiday
v3.0

Cover Photo © 2011 Ivan 'Doc' Holiday. All rights reserved - used with permission.

This book may not be reproduced, transmitted, or stored in whole or in part by any means, including graphic, electronic, or mechanical without the express written consent of the publisher except in the case of brief quotations embodied in critical articles and reviews.

Outskirts Press, Inc.
http://www.outskirtspress.com

ISBN: 978-1-4327-7089-1

Outskirts Press and the "OP" logo are trademarks belonging to Outskirts Press, Inc.

PRINTED IN THE UNITED STATES OF AMERICA

He who smiles instead of Rages.. is always Stronger....

— *Chinese Proverb*

Special Thanks

To my friends David & Ellen Lane of the World Famous Riverside Cafe in Vero Beach, Florida for their on going support and the publication of this book.

To my wife Shirley for 12 years of love, devotion and guidance.

To my son Caine for watching my back.

To my daughter Rianna for bringing out my softer side.

To my friends and cigar sponsor Wes & Vivian at Big Smoke, Ormand Beach, Florida.

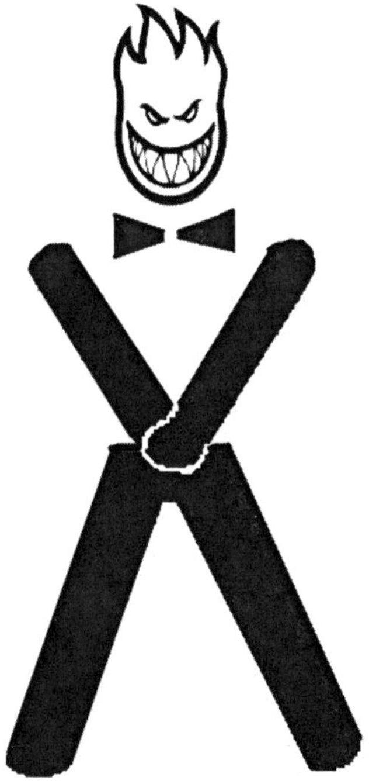

Table of Contents

Foreword
Chapter 1: 1
Chapter 2: 11
Chapter 3: 29
Chapter 4: 51
Doc's Scrapbook 57
Gone but never forgotten 78
Chapter 5: 82
Chapter 6: 106
Chapter 7: 119
The Ten Commandments of Bouncing 143
About the Author 144
Links 146

Foreword

My Dad and I first worked together at the Laconia Biker Rally in 2000. It was the proudest moment of my life. Seeing my old man standing up to a bunch of unruly bikers or just watching the faces of my fellow bouncers as they listened to every word my father said with respect and loyalty. When I think of me and my Dad, I think of the movie 'Rocky Balboa' and especially the part where Rocky and his son have it out on the street.

Rocky said *"I'd hold you up to say to your mother, "this kid's gonna be the best kid in the world. This kid's gonna be somebody better than anybody I ever knew." And you grew up good and wonderful. It was great just watching you, every day was like a privilege. Then the time come for you to be your own man and take on the world, and you did. But somewhere along the line, you changed. You stopped being you. You let people stick a finger in your face and tell you you're no good. And when things got hard, you started looking for something to blame, like a big shadow. Let me tell you something you already know. The world ain't all sunshine and rainbows. It's a very mean and nasty place and I don't care how tough you are, it will beat you to your knees and keep you there permanently if you let it. You, me, or nobody is gonna hit as hard as life. But it ain't about how hard ya hit. It's about how hard you can get it and keep moving forward.*

How much you can take and keep moving forward. That's how winning is done! Now if you know what you're worth then go out and get what you're worth. But ya gotta be willing to take the hits, and not pointing fingers saying you ain't where you wanna be because of him, or her, or anybody! Cowards do that and that ain't you! You're better than that! I'm always gonna love you no matter what. No matter what happens. You're my son and you're my blood. You're the best thing in my life. But until you start believing in yourself, ya ain't gonna have a life."

My father's life is like a Rocky story. Never giving up, always getting up when the bouncing trade beat him to his knees and tried keeping him there. Dad always said *"when I'm down in life or in the ring, I have this little voice in my head that tells me 'Get up and fight this guy hard', so that's what I do."* The old man is old school and hardcore.

I remember he told this guy that worked for him one time,

"I'm not disrespecting you bro. When I fuck your old lady, kick your dog's ass and smoke your stogies..that's disrespect."

Dad is one of a kind and I'm proud to say he's my father.

Last month, when we were filming our Reality TV show sizzle reel in Los Angeles, Dad told me,

"Son, I know we bang heads at times and don't see eye to eye most of the time..but at the end of the day you are still my son & I love you."

Caine Samson Arsenault

1

"The first draft of anything is shit"
- Ernest Hemingway

BOUNCER: (boun'sar) n.
1. a person or thing that bounces.
2. (slang) a person hired to remove very disorderly people from a nightclub, restaurant, etc. *Webster Newworld Dictionary*

I wish it was as simple as the dictionary explains but there's a lot more to it than that. Now in 2010 we have a bunch of British asshole's who never bounced, wanting to remove the word / term 'Bouncer' from the Oxford English Dictionary. They say the term is derogatory and insulting. Way I see it, the only insult is having idiots like these fucking wankers running their gators in a trade they never worked or split a drop of blood for. Last I heard the Oxford people told them to blow it out their ass. Anyway, on to more important matters. We find bouncers throughout ancient history. The significance of the doorman/bouncer as the person allowing (or barring) entry is found in a number of Mesopotamian myths (and later in Greek myths descended from them), including that of Nergal overcoming the seven doormen guarding the gates to the Underworld. This is like some serious 'Clash of the Titan's' shit! Even in the holy bible you got bouncers. In 1 Chronicle 26 of the Old Testament, the Levitical Temple is described as having a number of 'gatekeepers' - amongst their duties are "protect[ing] the temple from theft", from "illegal entry into sacred areas" and "maintain[ing] order", all functions they share with the modern concept of the bouncer, though the described temple servants also serve as holy persons and administrators themselves (it is noted that some administrative function is still present in today's bouncing in the higher position of the supervisor). In the time of the Romans there was a position known as the 'Ostiarius' (doorkeeper), initially a slave or other such inferior personage, who guarded the door, and sometimes ejected unwanted people from the house whose gate he guarded. The term later become a low-ranking clergy title. Plautus, in his play *Bacchides* (written approximately 194-184 BC), mentions a "large and powerful" doorman / bouncer as a threat to get an unwelcome visitor to leave. Then there was Tertullian, an early Christian author living mainly in the 1st century AD, while reporting on the casual oppression of Christians in Carthage, noted that bouncers were counted as part of a semi-legal underworld, amongst other 'shady' characters such as gamblers and pimps. When people ask me what I do for a living, I say I am hired to remove unruly patrons from places that serve alcohol. But that's just the tip of the iceberg, as you will come to understand as you read on. Bouncing is a job that wears many hats. Public Relations, security, fire safety, first-aid responder, mediator, liberator and protector.

I have been a bouncer for 29 years. Worked my first door at the Penalty Box Pub/The Forum Inn in Edmonton, Alberta,

Canada – March 8, 1982. My son Caine was born four months later. Today I have worked a total of 55 nightclubs and bars in both Canada and the US. This doesn't count the other 100 or so I worked in briefly, trained or just plain fucking quit after swallowing as much bullshit as I could take.

I have a medical record of 2 bullet wounds, 4 puncture wounds, 11 broken bones, 8 concussions and one poisoning. I've been shot in the ass with a 22 caliber rifle and hit in the left shoulder with 00 buck.

I've been cut with everything from broken bottles to a crackwhore's finger nails! I've been beat on, puked on, spit on, cigarette burned, threatened and cussed out. I've been hit with beer bottles, pool cues, bar stools, ashtrays, bar trays, woman's purses, lawsuits and child support! I've seen shit that would gag a maggot! N-a-s-t-y! Bro you ain't seen nasty. It was 1998 as I recall, I was bouncing at a side street bar in Daytona Beach, Florida called the 'Crooks Den'. It was owned by an old friend of mine Bill Crooks (R.I.P.) On a scale of 1 to 10 - it was a shithole. Well, I was bouncin' and bangin' a bartender we'll call "Barbie". Last thing I need is a pissed off blond MILF from the past who happens to be married to a ball busting lawyer. Anyway, this cracked out skank comes walking in and sits at the bar facing the large mirror that ran the length of the back wall. She and Barbie begin to have words. Barbie refused to serve her. As I walked up to escort the troll out, the bitch reaches under her jean skirt and pulls out a bloody tampon and throws it at Barbie behind the bar! I grabbed the bitch by the belt and the wrist of her bloody fingers and dragged the nasty whore out the back alley door. When I got back, Barbie was on fire!! None of the girl's would go near the bloody beaver plug, so I was elected to follow the red snail track down the mirror and behind the liquor bottles to find it. I found the little bastard stuck between a bottle of Jack Daniels and Old Crow. I used a pair of hotdog tongs to remove it and chucked tongs and all in the garbage. Hands down that is the nastiest shit I every came across. Like old Norm at the Beverly Crest Rock Bar in Edmonton, Alberta used to say, "That bitch is so nasty, she pours salt water down her pants to keep the crabs fresh!"

It was 1980 when I was first introduced to the world of bouncing.

I remember I was watching Laurence Tureaud aka 'Mr.T' in the Toughest Bouncer in America Contest March 25, 1980. Mr.T worked as a bouncer early in his career. It was at this time that he created the persona of Mr.T. In 1970, he legally changed his name to Mr.T. His wearing of gold neck chains and other jewelry was the result of customers losing the items or leaving them behind at the night club after a fight. Some asshole who may have been barred from the club or trying to avoid another confrontation would not re-enter the club if Mr.T wore their shit at the front door. When a customer returned to claim an item, it was readily visible and available with no further confrontations required. Along with controlling the violence as a doorman, Mr.T was mainly hired to keep out drug dealers and users. "*I knocked down the door with my shoulder and then I roughed up those six guys and the drug dealer. After that I had them arrested,*" Mr.T once said. During his bouncing days Mr.T was in over two hundred fights and was sued a number of times but won each case. "*I have been in and out of the courts as a result of my beating up somebody. I have been sued by customers whom I threw out that claimed that I viciously attacked them without just cause and/or I caused them great bodily harm as a result of a beating I supposedly gave them,*" Mr.T once remarked.

He eventually parlayed his job as a bouncer into a career as a bodyguard that lasted almost ten years. Working for the likes of Steve McQueen, Muhammad Ali, Leon Spinks, and Diana Ross.

But anyway, back to the Toughest Bouncer in America Contest shit. There were three events in the contest: The Bounce; where one had a 115 pound stunt man to throw as far as possible; The Blast; where you jumped from behind a bar, ran around a bunch of tables, jumped over a railing and smashed through a four inch wooden door to ring a bell behind that door stopping the clock. Finally, The Box; two men with the highest scores fought in a three-round boxing match to determine the overall winner.

Mr.T twice won this contest and has been an inspiration over the years. I have had the chance to admire him over this time and watch him go from bouncer, to bodyguard for the stars, to movie star in *Rocky III*. I've seen him help kids and devote his life to helping others less fortunate. Hell, he even had his own cartoon series! The Toughest Bouncer in America Contest only showed a small piece of a really big man. If you ask him what his real name is, he will tell you..

*"My first name is 'Mr,' my middle name is 'period,'
last name is 'T' "*

Today, when I look back on the contest after 29 years, I know it gave people the wrong impression about us; that bouncers were just a bunch of Neanderthals who work in bars and like to fight. I mean shit..back then in the Toughest Bouncer in America Contest you got a group of large men trying to see who can throw some little bastard the farthest on National television! As a matter of fact, the stuntman they were throwing suffered a broken collarbone when Mr.T threw him further than the landing mat! I even had to deal with it at home. My daughter Rianna was in grade two and told her class during a 'What is your daddy's job' day.. *"My daddy is a bouncer and beats up drunk people!"* God..I had to go to the school and explain to her class and teacher that I did not beat people up for a living.

I know Mr.T only did it to get recognition and it did just that. I don't blame him for it. Hell I just finished shooting a Bouncer Reality TV show (sizzle reel) in Los Angeles this week and I would imagine it will put me in a bad light at times. The old love-hate scenario...oh those fickle fans!! But the fact remains the only thing the contest did was to send the art of bouncing back into the stone ages. The people who invented the contest probably weren't bouncers and if they were, they weren't very good ones. I recall the words of Chet Ballanger, an old bouncer of 28 years and sparring partner of former boxing legend Sugar Ray Robinson,

"I would rather face a man tougher than me... than to face a man smarter!"

I would like to take this opportunity to acknowledge an old friend, former Canadian heavyweight boxing champion Ken Lakusta. Ken and I fought in the same Canadian Toughman Contest in Edmonton, Alberta, Canada back in 1979. He won the contest and in time, went on to become a great Canadian Champion. Kenny and his girlfriend used to come to the Cadillac Ranch in Edmonton, Alberta where I bounced with Karen McDonald and Bongo Bob. I watched Ken fight big name fighters like George Foreman, Larry Holmes, Tommy Morrison, Razor Ruddock and Trevor Berbick. He later went on to become a favorite sparring partner of former world heavyweight champion Iron Mike Tyson. Kenny was always a game fighter and never ducked a challenge. He came in my bar many times and was always a gentlemen. I admired the way he always took time to talk to the little guy. I always considered Ken a friend though we did not travel the same circles. He was patriotic Canadian and truly a people's champion.

The last time I saw Kenny was at a McDonalds in Edmonton, Alberta, having breakfast with his daughters. It's been a lot of years Kenny, but you'll always be a Champion in my books!

In 1989 while working at a western club called the OK Corral, in Edmonton, Alberta, Canada a movie came out starring Patrick Swayze and Sam Elliott called *Road House*. Marko and I went to see it and thought it was entertaining. Sam Elliott is my favorite actor anyway, I always liked his westerns. We had to laugh at the part where Dalton (Patrick Swayze) wanted $5,000 up front and $500 per night. I wondered if that was an eight or ten hour shift? For six months after the movie came out, we had guys coming into the bar looking to be *coolers** at five hundred dollars a night. Some were even willing to work for five hundred dollars a week. Marko tipped back his leather fedora hat and told one guy *"How about six bucks an hour and you can start by cleaning the puke off the bathroom floor.. welcome aboard – COOLER!"* My Mum always said, *"too much television will rot your brains!"* ROADHOUSE II: LAST CALL came out in 2006 and should have been called 'TRASH CALL' because it was not worth the fuckin' tape it was shot on. A total bag of shit, this piss poor sequel went to DVD faster than flies on a shit pile! Then there was a movie called *The Brainsmasher* starring "The Dice Man" Andrew Dice Clay, but we're not even going to go there!

**Cooler – A bouncer with many years of experience. The head of security at a nightclub or bar.*

IVAN 'DOC' HOLIDAY

The Bouncer's Bible is the gospel according to Doc Holiday. It is the story of my life and what I have learned in the business. 30 years – That's three decades of working the door brother! Like the Holy Bible, *"The Bouncer's Bible - 2nd Edition"* is the Old and New Testament. What the business was back in the day and what it is today.

Welcome to Bouncing 101 - The School of Hard Knocks!

I remember sitting on a bar stool in the club after it had closed. I had a bar-rag full of ice on my right eye and my head pounded like a New Years hangover. I sat there in a daze, watching the bar-back mop blood off the floor. I couldn't help but notice that what looked like chiclets gum scattered on the dance floor were in fact some poor bastard's dearly departed teeth. I closed my eyes and slowly rocked my stiff neck from side to side. Jake, an ex-marine and my bouncing partner came limping over wiping blood off his nose with what was left of his security shirt.

"*Who in the fuck volunteered us for this chicken shit outfit?*" he said.

"*Stand down soldier, it's a shitty job but somebody's gotta do it*" I replied. " *You look like shit dipped in misery*" Jake smirked.

"*Ya and you look like something the cat pissed on a buried.*" I replied as I fingered a loose tooth. "*I need a fuckin' office job*" Jake said touching his swollen lip. "*I'm just getting to fuckin' old for this shit Doc*" Jake stated as he pulled a bag of Redman out of his back pocket.

"*Thirty years old and over the hill*" I grinned. " *Twenty-nine bitch!*" Jake fired back as he packed a wad of chewing tobacco into his bruised cheek.

"*Fuck it, let's go get drunk*" I said getting up from the bar stool.

"*Whiskey bent and Hell bound*" Jake smiled and spit.

When people come to a bar lookin' for a fight talk's cheap and they ain't buyin' any. Yes seventy-five percent of the time you can talk a patron out. But the other twenty-five percent is all about TCB baby! Like I told one tree hugging faggot who felt that I was a little over zealous in my removal of a violent patron. " *It's a little hard to get all warm a fuzzy with a guy*

IVAN 'DOC' HOLIDAY

when he's hammering the dog shit out of some prick on the floor with a fuckin' bar stool" In the famous words of Ivan 'Doc' Holiday:

"*There's a Time To Talk and A Time To Rock!*"

2

"An eye for an eye leaves everybody blind."
- Ghandi

Over the years I've worked with a lot of good bouncers, but a hell of a lot more poor ones. It's like apples, one bad one in the barrel will spoil the rest! *What makes a good bouncer?* A person with an equal balance of physical and mental ability. *What makes a great bouncer?* A person who has complete control over both abilities. I guess you could say a great bouncer is just a grown up Boy Scout. My friends used to say,

> *"Doc, you're the Charles Bronson of bouncing, the last of the hard men"*

I remember watching a security tape at a club I worked in Memphis in 1994. I had just started with the club that week and two bouncers were talking at the corner bar.

"*What's the deal with this fuckin' Holiday guy. They say he's the best but I just don't see it*" the bigger bouncer said.

"*I wouldn't fuck with him*" the smaller bouncer replied. "*The boss said he saw him a couple years back at a club in Jackson,*

Tennessee. He snatched the glasses off a cowboy's face, hit him three times and put the specks back on the fucker before he hit the ground."

"*That's horse shit!*" the bigger bouncer replied.

"*Well maybe so, but they say those green berets are tough bastard's and that S.O.B. was probably workin' the door when you and I were shittin' green!*" the smaller bouncer said and walked away. The truth is, I did take the glasses and I did hit the man; but after he fell I stuck the glasses in his shirt pocket so he'd have them when he came too. As for the Green Berets, well I had one in boot camp but then so did everyone else.. lol

In the old days bouncers were 'hired by the pound'. The old timers figured the bigger the better. A lot of emphasis was put on size not only as a visual deterrent to anyone starting trouble but also having the ability to take care of business if push came to shove. As a matter of fact old Norm didn't hire me until I got into a fight outside his club with a couple of drunk assholes. I whooped them good but what really impressed him was the four RCMP* it took to get a set of handcuffs on me! When I got bailed out of jail next morning, I had a message on my answering machine and a job with that old bastard. So the rule of thumb was six foot plus, two hundred pounds plus. Well times have changed. Nothing upsets me more than talking to a guy looking for a job who in his own words *"Can really kick some ass!"* or nowadays it's *"I'm an MMA* Fighter."* I never hire people who say they are good fighters. I tell them,

> *"I need good bouncers, not good fighters..*
> *you're just a lawsuit waiting to happen partner."*

If you like to fight do yourself a favor and don't be a bouncer!

I got a better idea, join the UFC and become a professional MMA fighter.

Maybe you don't like the idea of getting the shit beat out of you in a fair fight. OK, how about you travel to China and party at a Hong Kong whorehouse for a week. Then you come back and tell everybody you fought in the Kumite! Worked for Frank Dux. Bottom-line is, we have way to many juiced-up ego driven assholes in the trade. Bouncing is about "Preventing and Stopping fights" not "waiting for a fight or starting one".

* RCMP – Royal Canadian Mounted Police
* MMA – Mixed Martial Arts
* UFC – Ultimate Fighting Challenge

In 1986, I was working at a club in Alberta, Canada. I had a kid working for me, 6'5", 265lbs, twenty years-old. He got in an argument with a regular customer and punched the much smaller man in the face breaking his nose. After talking to witnesses I fired him for being over excessive. I told him that he didn't have the right temperament for the trade. I told him in this business for every man you beat on, ten of his friends are going to have a problem with you. You abuse ten people, you've got a hundred guys gunning for you and a bouncer isn't a hard man to find. He told me where to get off and left. He got a job at another club on the other side of town and three months later the police dropped by to ask me some questions. I guess the guy I fired was leaving work at 3:30 a.m. when someone drove by and killed him with a 12 gauge shotgun. I felt bad for the kid and for his family. But then old Doc is no stranger to 12 gauge buckshot...

I was workin' a cowboy bar outside Helena, Arkansas back in 1995. You see I had to catch a fast train the fuck out of

IVAN 'DOC' HOLIDAY

Dodge a week earlier. I pissed off some Ghetto Rat Gangsta's at a strip club I was bouncing at in Memphis, Tennessee. Seems these GIT's didn't appreciate having my boot stuffed so far up there ass they spit boot polish! Anyway, I was workin' this hillbilly shithole when this fat bastard with four teeth and breath that came straight out of a monkey's asshole, started acting up. He threw a beer bottle at the bartender Louise, so me and the boy's jacked his shit outside. This Billybob toothed motherfucker weighed about four hundred pounds and smelled like shit in a day old diaper! He got all bent out of shape. He kept calling me a '*Fuckin' Yankee*' and pointing at the Rebel flag tattooed on his left arm. I was not about to explain to this rocket scientist the difference between a "Yankee" and a "Canuck".

After a bit he ran out of breath and left.

We closed two hour later. All the staff members said good night and left for their cars. I walked out to my Ford Ranger that was parked next to the backdoor. I rolled down the window and got in closing the door. All of a sudden..BOOM! Glass sprayed everywhere as my back window exploded! *"What the fuck!"* I yelled as I ducked down and slammed the truck into gear. A second boom sounded and then a third. It was only when I started to roar out of the bar parking lot that I realized that I was getting shot at. In my side mirror I could see the silhouette of a big fat cocksucker holding a shotgun as I was leaving. My left shoulder and back of my neck began to burn. Well to make a long story short, the fat bastard that I threw out came back with a 12 gauge shotgun to pump some 00 buck up my ass! But the story gets even better. I got the local horse doctor (who I was screwing) to pull 00 buck out of my neck and shoulder cause I had no insurance. Now for the real kick in the nuts. Mr. Hillbilly Fuck was married to the sheriff's wife's sister. So he got ten days in the county jail for careless discharge of a firearm! Everyday is just a role of the dice and snake eyes is just a way of life for old Doc. I know when it's time to get my ass the fuck out of Dodge..again. I packed my shit, showed my veterinarian sweetheart my appreciation in the hay loft (God that girl had an ass that could crack walnuts) and ended up in Caruthersville, Missouri working at a bar called "Woody's".

For about five years after my 'Deliverance' experience in Arkansas, I'd get responses like these ones from old friends and people I hadn't seen in a while.

- "Doc Holiday..Son-of-A-Bitch! I heard hillbillies done killed your ass in Arkansas!"
- "I'll be Goddammed..Doc Holiday..I thought you were dead!"
- "Jesus-H-Christ..last I heard you got your ass blown away in a biker bar in Little Rock!"
- "I heard you got shot in some shithole in Missouri!"

For the record :

> "I got shot..I ain't dead..and yes
> I was workin' a shithole in Missouri."

In the past and present I have had undercover cops pose as disorderly drunks to nab over-excessive bouncers. I've also had Narc's come in posing as customers trying to buy drugs in the club. Cops have a job to do and I respect that. As for drug dealers, I protect my own club. If you're selling drugs in my bar your going to be escorted to the "Talking Area" (the area with no security cameras) and believe me the only reason I flush the fuckin' toilet is to get the drugs down & the water out of your ears so you can understand what the fuck I am telling you!

Your kind is not welcome in my club! Once we have had our little talk, I escort your sorry ass to the parking lot and off the property. Needless to say I have never had a drug dealer call the police on me. Go figure. The other side of the coin is, unless I catch the dude selling with the drugs in hand, I don't accuse anyone. I don't lean on some idiot who has his own personal stash.

I just escort them from the club - period. I do not condone casual drug use nor would I create a 'Strong Arm' type security team. I just take care of club business in-house, to ensure the protection of my employer's staff, patrons and property. Furthermore, if you come into my bar for the sole purpose of hurting someone, you will be physically removed to the parking lot and arrested! I think its a good time for a little humor..

One Bike Week evening I saw my security had someone stopped at the front door. When I walked over I saw a guy wearing dark glasses. He had a walking cane and a dog in a harness. The dog was a black lab, acting real excited, going back and forth from side to side. The blind man said he wanted to come in and have a drink and by law he had a right to come in with his seeing eye dog. All Service dogs have the legal right to enter your establishment.

"*That's true Mister*" I said, "*but that dog of yours isn't trained very well. He seems nervous and jumpy. Can you make him sit?*" There is a clause in the Florida law in regards to unruly service dogs that states : (3e) A public accommodation may exclude or remove any animal from the premises, including a service animal, if the animal's behavior poses a direct threat to the health and safety of others. Allergies and fear of animals are not valid reasons for denying access or refusing service to an individual with a service animal. If a service animal is excluded or removed for being a direct threat to others, the public accommodation must provide the individual with a disability the option of continuing access to the public accommodation without having the service animal on the premises.

So this guy was tugging on the harness saying, "*Sit boy..sit!!*" The dog just kept on sniffing the ground and going from side to side. This dog was wired! "*You know what I think mister? I think you're a cop and that's a drug dog*" I said. "*And unless you have a warrant, you and your girlfriend here are not allowed on the property.*" The cop ripped off his sunglasses, "*fuckin' smart ass*" and pulled the dog off down the street. Don't get me wrong, old Doc is Pro Law Enforcement but I am hired to protect my boss's best interests within the confines of the law. Loyalty is the backbone of the bouncing business. A bouncer is a professional hired to protect his boss's employees, customers and property. Thus my '4 P's of Bouncing' - "*Protection of Personnel, Patrons and Property*".

A good bouncer is a team player. Combined with the other security personnel they keep everybody safe and the bar under control. The overall goal is to protect your boss's investment so his establishment can make as much money as possible and his customers have a good time.

Safety is the most important factor in Bouncing.

There is no Protection without Safety 1st!!

I've always said bouncers can indirectly make or break a club. No one wants to party in a place where the security has a bad reputation for being over-excessive and intimidating customers. Where the bouncers start more fights than they prevent. This kind of behavior will eventually draw the wrong kind of crowd. In the last ten years I have seen the development of what I call a 'Bouncer Mafia'. You got a crew of fucking ego driven jerkoffs running the club and the management's ass is sucking wind.

They control the club's patrons, staff and management with fear tactics and criminal behavior. For example, starting fights to make management think they are needed. Having their buddies start fights with patrons they don't like. Allowing drug dealer's or prostitutes sell their shit in the club for a percentage. Letting in minors for sex or money. Stealing patrons money and/or valuables when they are over-intoxicated or passed out. The shit gets deep brother, that's why ninety percent of the time when I have to clean up some shithole I start by firing the bad bouncers first. Then I fix the trouble making patrons after. Like a tell my boys,

"If its got tits or tires..your bound to have a problem with it!"

When people come to a bar to fight they usually come prepared. They know there will be bouncers and are ready for them by means of concealed weapons or just shear numbers. Some years back in Canada, there was a thing called a "BOUNCER BASH". Three guys would come in and sit at a table; five minutes later four guys entered and would sit in the back; ten minutes later three more guys would come in and start to shoot pool; ten minutes more, three other guys came in and sat at the bar. All of a sudden the first three guys that came in started causing trouble at their table. The bouncers responded in force, four bouncers and a cooler. When security tried to remove the three trouble makers they were ambushed from behind by ten more punks. You see, all the guys that came in knew each other and had planned the attack.

Now you've got thirteen punks against five bouncers and one big problem!

It usually lasted about ten minutes but you ended up with a trashed bar and badly hurt security. I once got a broken left wrist and three cracked ribs out of a Bouncer Bash in 1989! This is a good example of the wrong kind of crowd. You see bouncers are like old time gunfighters. You get a reputation as a fighter and certain people are going to want to make a name for themselves by stomping a mud hole dry in your ass!

The end result is you're going to draw fighters to your club and sooner or later into your personal life.

In the early 1980's, a recession made it hard to find steady work in Canada, so I started fighting Toughman contests. I'd travel around to bars that hosted Toughman events in their clubs. Later on, I also got involved with illegal underground 'knuckling'. This is bare fist boxing which has been around since the early 1800's. It involved heavy betting and big payouts. Weight classes are determined by the fighters. If you figured you could whoop the guy's ass and he agreed to let you try, the fight was on and the bets slapped down. The rules were simple, you can only strike above the belt, fists only, no rounds or time limits. On the side lines the organizers watch for a fair fight. Anyone who broke the rules of combat was labeled a coward and a cheat and therefore was removed by four large men with wooden boatman clubs. Needless to say cheating didn't happen often. If you think that this was not much of a sport compared to the MMA think again my friend. There is no grappling or taking him to the ground to avoid punches and conserve strength. No time to feel your opponent out during the fight. No pre-fight information or fight tapes to review.

No ring doctor to say you had enough and no bell to save your ass. Zero Tap-outs in this game son. You go down, you best stay down! You get hurt, your corner man (who is usually a friend) is in charge of your money and carting your ass to the hospital should shit go south. To avoid being booed by the crowd and/or removed by the large gentlemen with the boatmen clubs, one was quick to set a steady pace of punches per minute and try to maintain it. The MMA is like the cobra versus the mongoose. Knuckling is like the cobra versus the cobra! I was fighting about once or twice a month depending on how hard my fights were and how bad I needed the money. A few months later, guys started coming to my bar to try me. It got to the point where they would wait for me in the parking lot after work with cash in hand. When I refused to fight and avoided them, they would fight with my friends and regulars from the bar. Sometimes they would start fights in the bar. I was forced to leave town because of my street fighter reputation. My friend Panhead Rick once said,

"A man spends half his life building a reputation and the other half trying to get away from it."

What kind of people become bouncers? Well, most of them are guys who have day jobs but are looking to make some extra cash. There are those who work as bouncers because their family owns or manages the club or bar. Some guys do it for the chance to be a figure of authority and shit on people. I call these guys 'Power Trippers'. They're like rent-a-cops without the uniforms. Most of these guys have an alligator mouth with a canary ass and couldn't break a grape in a food fight! Then there are the guys who do it to improve their love lives and pick up woman. I call these gems, 'Casanova's'. They go though the bar kissing every female's cheek and the boss's ass!

These pussy hounds are too busy chasing ass to do their job.

Next are the 'Juice Monkeys'. These are the local gym rats who spend every waking moment pumping tons of iron and stackin' juice (Anabolic Steroids). The end result; big muscles and a bad attitude to compensate for a small dick! I'm not saying that all steroid enhanced individuals are bad.

Today fuckin' ninety percent of our professional athletes have taken or still take performance enhancing drugs. What great role models for our up and coming teen athletes!

Bottom-line is, you need to be smart when you venture into this type of endeavor. Knowledge is Power! Know the risks and make smart choices.

If you're going to do it, do it the right way and talk to a licensed Medical Doctor. Roid Rage is no joke. I had this one gorilla working with me, hammered full of testosterone cypionate, who jumped over top of two fellow bouncers and began to choke a patron being escorted to the door. It's pretty sad when bouncers have to physically restrain one of their own!

There was one steroid-junkie who got all bent out of shape one night because I told him that he would have to wait outside the club for his girlfriend, who was a dancer. The dude took to trying to intimidate me with his size. *Smart like tractor...strong like bull!* I said in my best Arnold Schwarzenegger accent. He got real upset about that. By this time his girlfriend came out and tried to calm him down but he was more determined now because he had a few dancers to show off for.

"Bring your white ass outside..cracker!" he said and punched the door.

"What are you going to do, benchpress me to death?" I replied.

He was a black male in his early twenties, about six foot, two hundred and twenty-five pounds.

"*You're lucky the cops are here.*" I said looking over his shoulder as I stepped outside the door. When that ignorant bastard turned his head to look at the empty parking lot, I kicked him square in the balls dropping him like a bad habit! His girlfriend got pissed off at him and left with another dancer, leaving the mighty Jerkcules curled up on the sidewalk with a bad case of swollen gonads! I guess you could say she left him holding the bag!! A group closely related to the juice monkey's I refer to as 'Little short fuckers'. These are bouncers who are way too short for the trade, like four foot fuck-all to 5'5". Not only can they not see in a crowd but they can't be seen. Add to this a serious case of 'Napoleon' or 'Little Man Syndrome' and you end up with something that looks like a pro linebacker with his legs cut off! Add 'Roid Rage' to the mix and you got a pumped up yard gnome pissed off at the world who wants to screw every chick over 5'6" and beat up every guy over six foot!

Bottom-line is, I never hire a bouncer under 5'10" if I can help it.

There is another group of winners I like to call the Fun boys, bouncers that drink and party harder than the customers. These idiots get canned quick! Think about it for a minute, you got some ass clown who wants to work as a bouncer and get paid with a free bar tab! RED FLAG! And last but not least, the cream of the crop: Ex-con's and Felons that have a violent past and habitual criminal traits. They work as bouncers because they know that the clubs don't do criminal background checks. This is a major problem in our trade today. I'm not saying that I guy doesn't deserve a second chance but a fucking sex offender or violent ex-con has no place working security in a bar or nightclub period!

Ninety percent of the time when I am called to clean up a bar or club, I fire half the bouncers because they can't pass a criminal background check!

Its like I tell fucking dumbass club owners,

"Would hire a pedophile to watch your kids? Then why would you hire a violent felon to protect your patrons!"

You know, some of my best bouncers have been good old country boys off the farm and ex-military veterans. If a person has the right size and the right attitude, I can train him or her to do the job and do it well. You see I have come across a shitload of tough guys over the years. Guys who like to fight and love confrontation. But there always comes that one night when the tough guy gets a serious ass whooping. Most of them decide that they need to find another line of work and quit.

"To fight and conquer in all our battles is not supreme excellence; supreme excellence consists in breaking the enemy's resistance without fighting"
- Sun Tzu

I had a friend Steve Anados that worked for me back in 1997 at the Harley Rendezvous's Knockers Club in upper New York State.

Steve was a professor of Physic's at the University of Albany and a damn good bouncer. He was nice enough to give me a tour of his college and show me the Leaner Particle Accelerator. Beam me up Scotty, there's no intelligent life forms in this bar!! Over the years, I've tried to get through the heads of these tight ass employers: if you pay six bucks an hour to your security and have six bouncers, you might get lucky and have one guy who's worth a rat's ass and the others are just a waste of space that could be used for paying customers. Do you really think bouncers are going to put their ass's on the line for forty bucks a night! Yes some boys are not the sharpest tools in the shed but then they all aren't window licker's on the short bus either! In the words of Joe 'Peckerhead' Wyse *"If I had shit in my right hand and your security in my left hand at least when the trouble started I'd have something in my right hand I could throw!"* When hiring security, go for Quality not Quantity! I suggest you take your six bucks an hour, make it ten bucks an hour and hire three professional bouncers. With that kind of cash you're going to have your pick of some pretty good security. Just be careful. If I had a dollar for every peckerwood that said he was a professional cooler, I'd be retired in the Virgin Islands with harem full of high school cheerleaders! I know for a fact that most bar owners are so goddam tight with their money that they would fuck a dead whore in the beer cooler just to get their money's worth out of the bitch. But if you are an employer reading this book here's some advice: take good care of your bouncers and they will take good care of you.

It's like chess, you can't venture out to capture your opponents King until you protect your own. Bouncers are hired to protect you & your investment. The next time you see a bouncer standing there, think of your local firemen. They sit around the fire station playing cards and getting paid for it out of our taxes but when a four-alarm fire hits these men are there to put their ass's on the line for us. It really burns my ass when I see employers hire prison guards or police officers as bouncers.

I am Pro-Law Enforcement...don't get me wrong but I never hire any type of Law Enforcement , retired or otherwise. Reason being, they are trained under a totally different protocol. Law Enforcement are trained under an "Authoritative Protocol" . Bouncers must be trained under an "Affirmative Protocol". In layman's terms, Cops can arrest and boss people around. Bouncers have no more rights than a regular citizen and must learn to work within these limitations. Like I say,

"When cops become bouncers...Patrons become Perps!"

When I see uniformed police working at a nightclub and

"You a bounty hunter?" the stranger asked.

"Not really. You could say I do a little bit of everything." cowpoke stated.

"Well then, you're what I call a Jack of all Trades." replied the stranger not looking up from his whiskey.

"Yup, that's me all right." the cowpoke said sticking out his chest with pride. The bounty hunter raised his head and looked the guy straight in the face with a set of gravestone eyes.

"Then I strongly suggest you leave the work to a professional."

You never hire gangs or gangsta's to work as bouncers.

If you want a good example of this, try the Rolling Stones concert in Altamont, California back in the 70's when they hired the 'Angels' to work band security. I have the utmost respect for the Hells Angels and I have friends who are members but I would never let them work for me! Lets just say that 1% motorcycle club members don't have the 'Patience or Restraint needed to deal with some drunk patron running his mouth.'

Another pet peeve of mine are D.J.'s that like to play bouncer. Stay in your booth, spin your fuckin CD's and leave the trouble to security. If the security is short-staffed they will let you know. Just keep your eyes on the crowd and report any potential trouble. While I'm on the subject of dumbass D.J.'s... never let a D.J. yell over the microphone "Fight..Fight!"

Last thing you need is a call to arms that could insight a riot! Lets just spin CD's and shit on the dumb fuck's who want to hear 'Freebird'!

I remember a D.J. at a strip club I worked in New York. We had a pushing match between two girls and a few customers. Just as I got the people involved calmed down, Mr. DJ shows up pointing a finger and putting his two-cents worth in, which started the whole thing up again. By the time I got that dickhead muzzled and back in his booth, we found that someone had ripped off an expensive portable CD deck and two full CD cases. Approximately $1,500 gone!! Now today with everything digital and on laptops...its even more goddamn expensive.

I like live music if the band doesn't suck like a crackwhore on the devil's dick. Funniest thing I ever heard was a buddy of mine Jeremy, who was playing with 24-Steven at the Riverside Cafe. This drunk broad kept pestering him to play some ZZ-Top. He finely had enough and told the chick *"Do I look like a Fucking Jukebox to you!!"* Funny as hell!!

I am a professional Cooler, it's all I do and I do it because I love the trade and enjoy working with people. I remember back in the day when I was single..When I was on a date and sitting in a club, I had a bad habit of watching the people. You can take the bouncer out of the bar, but you can't take the bar out of the bouncer. I had to keep apologizing to my date. She thought I was not interested in her because I keep glancing around the bar as she was speaking to me. No wonder I never had a girlfriend for very long in those days! Today, my wife Shirley looks around and watches people as much as I do!!

Twenty-one years ago my mother asked me why I liked bouncing. I thought for a moment and said, "when people work hard all week at their jobs they come home, shower, put on their best clothes, and go to a club to have fun. I get paid to help these people have a good time. You gotta love it.." I believe God gives everyone a gift and I guess mine is being a bouncer. I have been told that pound for pound I'm the best cooler in the business by the people I serve. Today with almost thirty years under my belt, I am accepted worldwide as the leading authority in Nightclub & Bar Security. I like it when a customer shakes my hand and tells me I'm the best bouncer he's ever met because the night before I didn't throw him out when he got a little loud and I got him a cab home when he was too drunk to drive. If I accidentally bump someone I tell them I'm sorry. If I spilled their drink, I replace it. If I have to tell someone to stop doing something I feel is wrong, I always smile and say thank you after the person complies to my request.

Some people ask me, *"Aren't you a little short to be a bouncer?"* I just smile and say, *"It's easier to pull over a tree, than it is to push over a stump."* But hell I'm still 5'7" in my boots! You got to love people to be in this business. You have to be a social person who likes to work with people. But on the other hand, like it or not we are in the asshole business. Unlike a proctologist, we don't make half the cash and when we put our foot up their ass, they ain't sleepin! Fact in point.

Being a bouncer is many things to many people and every town has a bouncer who thinks he's tough as a nickel steak but every strength has and 'needs' its weakness. As it is with the Taoist philosophy of Yin & Yang. It is impossible to talk about yin or yang without some reference to the opposite, since yin and yang are bound together as parts of a mutual whole. For example; you cannot have the back of a hand without the front. Yin and yang transform each other, like an undertow in the ocean, every advance is complemented by a retreat, and every rise transforms into a fall. Thus it is my philosophical believe that bouncing is a 'Balance of Opposites..." Now that's deep man!!

> *"Heroes take journeys, confront dragons,
> and discover the treasure of their true selves"*
> \- Carol Lynn Pearson

3

"Life is hard; it's harder if you're stupid."
- John Wayne

I was working at a club up north fourteen years ago, where this bouncer had on Camo baseball hat, a pair of leather fingerless gloves and a two foot long steel maglite. This dude looked like Larry the Cable Guy's twin brother! He was supposedly the Head of Security but all I saw was a fuckin' clown with an attitude. I love the way this beefcake would walk around slapping the butt end of the flashlight into his empty hand to make a snapping noise. I wondered if it would make the same sound when I stuffed it up his ass and snapped off the handle! Ohhh…GET-ER-DUN!!

Every time a good looking chick came over to talk to me, he'd come over trying to put the cock block on old Doc. If he wasn't so fucking stupid he might of figured out that I was the backdoor man jackhammer-in' his old lady's love hole!

"Hello, I'm Ivan Holiday but my friends just call me Doc" I said walking up to a group of people he had just got through eye fucking. I shook hands with the four men saying, *"Don't mind that redneck with the big light and the small dick. He was just born a hemorrhoid and grew bigger!"*

They laughed and glanced over at Larry.

I thanked them for their business and ordered them a round on me.

"*Just ignore that fuckin' idiot* " I said. "*If you shoved his brain up an ant's ass it would roll around like a BB in a boxcar! Hell, I asked him yesterday why he wears that stupid ball cap all the time. When he lifted it up, there was a little green frog sittin' on his head.*"

"*What the fuck is that?*" I asked.

"*Fuck if I know*" the frog said. "*It started out as a wart on my ass!*"

Those guys laughed so hard I thought they were going to puke.

For the rest of the night, every time they saw the Larry the Cable Guy they fuckin' lost it! A person that has good temperament usually has a fair amount of self-control. Verbal abuse just comes with the territory. I mean if I kicked the shit out of every dickhead who copped an attitude with me, I'd be going though a fuckin' pair of boots every weekend!

A bouncer has to be able to take cheap talk with a grain of salt.

You usually get it from some pissed off bitch-with-a-dick or some clown talking out of his ass who couldn't fight for Breast Cancer!

Any recruit straight out of bootcamp can tell you first hand about verbal abuse. If a patron's remarks are getting out of hand take the person to one side or outside and talk with them. When the verbal abuse comes to a point where it needs to stop, show up in force and tell the asshole to hit the bricks. If he bucks on you..jack his shit! That's how it's done son.

It's absolutely impossible to reason with an angry drunk person, whose eyes look like two eagle's assholes in a power dive! Corporal Walsh once told me, *"The secret is to keep your cool when everybody else around you is losing theirs."* Bottom-line is security cannot be disrespected or your function in the club becomes a joke. If a patron will not calm down and conduct themselves accordingly, they are removed from the premises - Period. But sometimes there are exceptions..

    I was running a crew at a strip club in Albany, N.Y. called Knockers back in 1997, a man in the club with four other guys sat his drink on the stage. I asked him to please remove his drink.

    "Don't worry about it" he said. *"It could spill and cause a dancer to fall"* I replied. *"Don't worry about it"* he said again. I walked around the stage and he picked up his drink.

    He stared me down and called me a dick. I just smiled and walked away. The manager was going to have him removed, but I said no. I got another one of my bouncers to work that section. The guy was around fifty-five years-old and had something to prove to his son and friends. I told the boss after work the man had a wad of Ben Franklin's on him and I bet he spent five thousand dollars in the club during that rally weekend. *"I'm not here to make friends J.C."* I told the manager. *"I'm here to make money."*

    A bar is the number one place where people come with their problems. Everybody has personal problems in their life but it's just not good to bring yours to work with you. In the Special Forces a soldier learns to turn off their emotions and take care of the business at hand.

    To give 100% toward the mission and the team. Bouncing is the same thing. How do you expect to handle a hot situation in the bar when you're in a bad mood and pissed off at the world! Keep a clear head. Keep your mind on the job at hand and be alert! I always tell my guys to try and get a two hour nap in before work because by three am when you hit the wall you're going to need it. I tell my boys, working for me is like playing for a professional football team. When you show up, have your head in the game and your shit together. We got six to eight hours that you need to do your job and support your brothers. Your not worth a fuckin dime to me if your body is on the floor and your mind is thinking about the fight you and your girlfriend just had before you came to work. Do you think a pro quarterback is thinking - *'wonder what cheerleader I'm gonna fuck tonight?'* NO. He's thinking about the 300lb defensive end that wants bury his ass in the AstroTurf! Be a + plus to your security team, not a - minus. Your paid to do the job..So do it good and do it right!

Anger is like a stick of dynamite. Your temper is the fuse and your 'temperament' is the length, and only as long as the fuse. A tired bouncer has a very short fuse! As I told the group at my UK TOUR seminar in London last year,

> *"You see its not how long it takes for you to lose your cool..but rather, how long it takes you to get it back under control and the damage done in between." - Ivan 'Doc' Holiday*

Remember old Doc's - 'ABC's of Bouncing' – (A)lways (B)e (C)ool.

A bouncer who has a girlfriend working in the same bar is just trouble waiting to happen. As a rule of thumb, I never hire a bouncer and his girlfriend to work in the same bar. Like I told you before, keep your personal life out of the bar. I can't count the number of times I have seen a bouncer and his girlfriend standing in the kitchen or outside arguing or watched a bouncer start a fight with a patron because he was hitting on his girlfriend who was drinking in the bar. The bottom line is I don't give a flying fuck who you are..unless you're a fuckin' pimp, if some piece of shit grabs a mitt full of your old lady's ass, you're going to pound that mother-fucker into sawdust! There are exceptions to every rule. I've seen older couples work a bar together and be all right with it. But it's like snake handling, you show me a snake handler who has never been bit and I'll show you a woman that doesn't bitch!

Take my advice, if you want to end a good relationship let your wife or girlfriend frequent the bar where you work. Women love to talk shit in the bathroom. You know what happens to teenagers that like to gossip and start rumors in high school? They grow up to become drama queens and douchebag divas in the local nightclubs! Like saber tooth crotch crickets on a set of hairy balls..they are relentless! If they can't find shit to talk about, they just make it up. Believe me, they'll talk shit to anybody stupid enough to believe their crap! While we're on the subject, I don't like boyfriends of the female employees hanging around either. So many times I've watched some silicone cinderella sucking face with her Ken doll boyfriend like she's in a fuckin' porno and at the end of the night can't understand why her tips are shit!! Take it from the Legend, if a bouncer can't pickup a piece of ass in a bar at closing time, he couldn't get laid in a fuckin' whorehouse with a hundred dollar bill taped to his forehead! A lot of babes dig bouncers, but just get a phone number or tell her to meet you at the local 7-11 or IHOP after work. Never let people see you leave the bar with a midnight snack, unless you want your shit posted on Facebook before your next shift! Loose lips - sink ships! Camera phones and texting – If picture paints a thousand words and your ass is done!

A bouncer never touches alcohol or drugs while he is

working. There are no exceptions to this rule. If you have to report an incident to police and they smell alcohol on your breath, you're going to have a hard time getting any kind of respect from a police officer. If someone buys you a drink, have it put on ice until after work - unopened! I never accept an open drink from someone you don't know.

If you accept a nonalcoholic drink from a person make sure it is unopened or from the establishment. If you leave your drink for some reason, when you come back pour it out and get a new one. I am a real hard ass when it comes to this and I will tell you why. I once had someone drop micro-dot acid in my coffee. Within minutes, I felt my skin start to crawl and I was sweatin' like a whore in church! When the dance floor strobelights came on, I lost my balance and hit the floor with a heart rate of two hundred beats per minute! When the EMT's arrived, they hooked me up to an IV and took me to the local hospital. Getting a tube shoved down your throat to pump out your guts is not a good time. My body ached all over and I had stomach cramps like I swallowed barbwire!

Bottom-line : Be alert and never drop your guard..Expect the Unexpected!

A bouncer is usually the first person a customer encounters when he or she enters a club. This is why it is important for a bouncer to dress and carry himself well. Dress with pride, you are representing the club. If you want to command respect from your patrons, then dress like a fuckin professional and not a goddamn homeless person. I have seen bouncers wearing security shirts that look like they dug it out of a dumpster!

I told this bouncer one time who showed up late for work, (but early enough to get his ass fired!) "I'd like two security shirts just like the one you're wearing son...yup..one to shit on and the other to cover it up with!"

A security team needs to be dressed the same and in uniform. By uniform I don't mean a fuckin' Rent-A-Cop monkey suit. I mean proper attire that looks the same. Think what would happen if football teams all wore that same colors..are you with me on this, slim!

On my UKTOUR in November 2010, I told the brothers over in England the same thing. They love to wear Black. Worst fuckin' color a bouncer can where. How in the fuck do you expect me to see my team mates in a dark nightclub when they are all wearing black. Biker bars are even worse. Every swinging dick in the fuckin joint is wearing black leather!

Pay attention to what I am sayin son or I'll slap you so hard you'll starve to death before you stop slidin'. Bouncers need to be seen! If I wanted undercover bouncers, I'd fucking hire James Bond 007! If I needed a crew that couldn't be seen in the dark, I'd hire fuckin Ninja's!!

I tried to explained this to the European boys..Black is a sinister color!!

1 - What color roses does the mafia send to you when they are going to kill your ass? - BLACK.
2 - What color is a hitman's leather gloves? - BLACK.
3 - Satan's church holds what type of mass? - BLACK.
4 - Bad Magic is _ _ _ _ _ Magic? - BLACK.

If you don't see a pattern here son, your a few french fries short of a happy meal! Also while on tour, I ran into not only black security jackets but matching black military fatigues/pants and black combat boots! Hell why not just shave your heads and hang a fuckin picture of Adolf Hitler at the front door! Patrons get a little intimidated when surrounded by a bunch large men dressed like neo-Nazi's.

A bouncer wants to be viewed as a 'Protector'. We are in the PROTECTION BUSINESS. We want our patrons and employee's to feel save when we are on the job. We want to present a friendly, 'approachable' demeanor. Always willing to listen and assist our patrons and staff members.

While on the topic, I don't allow my bouncers to wear shirts with cut off sleeves or tank tops, this ain't the goddam beach! Also I don't want a bouncer wearing a fuckin' security shirt, three sizes to small. No, it doesn't make you look bigger, it makes you look stupid!

It's like watchin' a retard eatin' hot-wings and tryin' hard not to laugh!

Do you want patrons to think you sold your security shirt from your little sister's closet? Let's stop kicking this dead horse and continue on..

I hate to see a bouncer wearing leather gloves or dark sunglasses inside a club to look tough. Even worse are bouncers who wear fingerless sap gloves, spiked wrist bands, two foot long steel flashlights, collapsible steel batons, pepper spray,stun guns or displaying anything to make the statement *'I am a bad ass motherfucker'*!

Did you know that having large rings on every finger and punching someone with that same hand, can be considered assault with a dangerous weapon!

I worked at a biker bar in upper New York where a bouncer carried a six-inch ka-bar army knife on his belt. I walking up to the six foot four inch bouncer, looked him in the eye and said, *"Nice knife."*

He reached down to show me his blade but the case was empty and I was holding his knife. He was really surprised!

I told him in a fight if a police officer goes down on the ground his hands go to cover his weapon. He knows if his attackers get his gun he's in deep shit! It is bad enough that some people carry concealed weapons in a bar, we as bouncers don't want to be promoting it.

In certain clubs I wear my bullet proof vest. Especially if I am called to a club to clean the place up and it has a history of weapon or gang violence.

They're a good idea but remember this important fact, keep the vest a secret and concealed as possible. Once someone knows you are wearing one you will lose the advantage the vest provides.

Never wear a security shirt made of material that is too hard to tear. Never wear a tie unless it is clip on and never wear a Bolo tie of any kind. Jewelry should be left at home unless you're sure it won't be lost in a scuffle. Wear loose comfortable clothing but not baggy or sloppy in appearance. Always wear a belt! If you want to wear your pants down around your thighs too show your homies or homo's –whichever- that you're pimp, fly and lookin' for a gay guy..best you find another line of work. A bouncer must be able to move without being restricted by tight clothing or pants hanging off his ass! If you work at a white shirt and tie club, go to the local thrift shop to buy your shirts. People donate great second hand dress shirts and you can buy them for about ten bucks a shirt. You can buy a dozen and never have to worry about getting it ripped in a fight or spilling coffee on it. Try to wear a shirt a size bigger than your normal size. It makes it hard for someone to size you up. The element of surprise is very useful in the bouncing business and being underestimated can give a person a considerable advantage.

Never underestimate an opponent. Male or female, big or small, remember you don't need to be big to pull a trigger.

My grandfather once told me,

IVAN 'DOC' HOLIDAY

*"The west separated the men from the boys..
but Sam Colt made them equal!"*

Long hair can be a real problem in a fight. If you do have long hair, always wear your hair in a braid or ponytail. Make sure that it doesn't hang down in your face and hinder your vision. While you're working, use a gel to make your hair slippery and hard to get a grip on in a fight.

Matter a fact, getting dragged off the bed by the beard is no fun either is it Panhead Rick. Dumb bastard! That Tonya the Treasure Troll was a fuckin' hoot! All I had to do was get her drunk and tell her Panhead Rick had some blonde on the back of his bike. That bitch would get hotter than to squirrel's fuckin' in a wool sock! She was a firecracker that girl and wilder than a fifth ace. Anyway back to bouncing.

Footwear should be lace up and flat soled, steel toed if possible. A lot of guys wear cross-trainers while others wear a hiking boot style. Avoid wearing boots that are loose, have high heels or smooth bottoms.

Bad footwear is a real disadvantage in a fight. Just ask this asshole who was the personal bodyguard of a well known Canadian boxing champion Danny Stonewalker. He came into the OK Corral back in 1989 with a couple of girls just before closing time and started showin' his ass. When I asked him to stop causing trouble or leave, he flicked his cigarette in my face and shouted "Fuck you white-ee". Talking time was over and I was pissed.

"Outside Cochise!" I growled. We eye balled each other as we made our way out the door. It was minus -30 and colder than a well digger's ass. I was wearing combat boots and noticed he had cowboy boots on. When I saw this, I forced the former Canadian Kick boxing Champion off the sidewalk and on to the icy parking lot. It was all over but the crying for the Bruce Lee wanna-be when I blocked a high kick and he slipped and fell.

It was Hockey Night in Canada and the gloves were off!

I was on that motherfucker like a mongoose on a snake's ass! I pulled his sweater over his head and started jack hammering the uppercuts! The end result was a one way ticket to the hospital for Geronimo with a broken jaw and a couple of teeth missin'. I definitely put a stop to his nasty smoking habit! OK, before we go any further I know it looks like a bouncer gets into a lot of fights. Well we do depending on how rough and tough the club is. But remember our job is to STOP fights not join in on the action!

Let it be known - I hate fighting and I detest violence. I like boxing but this is not fighting, it is a sport.

Uncle Tommy had this kid about sixteen show up at the boxing club one day. The kid said *"I want to learn how to fight."* Uncle Tommy said,

"I can't teach you how to fight son but I can teach you how to box...and a boxer will beat a fighter hands down every time."

While we are on the subject of fighting, it seems the more you avoid physical confrontation the more it happens..go fuckin figure.

But then I don't have to be bouncing to end up in a bucket of shit.

Lee, I'm sorry but I have to throw you under the bus and tell this story.

Yes we are still brothers...and yes I am still pissed off!

I was visiting brother Lee, an old bouncer from back in the day when we were young, dumb and full of cum. We were bullshitting and fuckin the dog when in come three motorcycle gang members. These guys were a small local 2% club trying to make a name for themselves.

Anyway, Lee tells me *"Doc back me up."*

I looked over at Lee, *"Are you fuckin' wacked bro"* I whispered.

"Just call John Law and trespass the fuckers."

"Fuck no..they roll up in my club and disrespect me by flying colors, they're gonna turn their cuts!" Lee growled.

"Flip - there - colors..are you fuckin' nuts!" I argued.

"I don't want the boss to think I'm too old to handle shit in here Doc.."

"Too old to handle shit? You gotta be.." before I could say one more word, Lee turned and walk down the two steps into the pool room area. *"Fuck..shit in a bear's ass!!"* I mumbled as I looked at the red haired bartender with the worried look on her face. I took the first step and to my left seated at a table was a short fat biker with a beard talking to a tall skinny tattooed bitch. It was at this time, the three 2% peckerwood's jumped Lee. Now I am no fucking dummy when it comes to a bar fight. Old Doc is undefeated in the 'tough old bastard' division. Why? Is it because I am a skilled martial artist? Fuck no! Its because, I am hands down the dirtiest streetfighter that ever bit down on a biker's balls! Thus, I all ready took a running inventory of all the shit I could use as a weapon. It was a short bar-stool on my right that I grabbed and nailed the first 2% biker with. He never seen it coming. He took out one bar table, two tall bar chairs and a drunk bystander on his way to the floor. By this time I figured I was gonna do quite well and on my way to sweet victory, till that fat bearded bastard with the tattooed skank jumped me from behind.

I guess he was just an asshole looking to impress his woman.

We slammed against the bar and I dropped the stool as the fatman had me in a choke hold. It was at this time one of the

2% biker's left Lee and punched me in the face. I could taste the blood in my mouth as the fucker's second swing hit the fat bastard's elbow! I could see the asshole hurt his knuckles as he gritted his teeth in pain. It was at this moment I reached back and grabbed a full beer off the bar top and layed it up the side of Mr. Broken-knuckle's fucking head! Beer sprayed down my arm as the 2% jerkoff hit the floor! The fatman choking me tried to get my swinging beer bottle arm locked up. Big Mistake! I turned and put both my feet up against the bar and pushed hard sending me and the fatman backwards into his old lady, table and chairs. The skinny bitch went flying along with the beer bottles. The table and chairs fell over as the fat bastard and I slammed on to the floor. He loosened his grip on me and I took full advantage driving a hammer fist past my leg down into his balls! I heard the buffalo-ass grunt like a pig as I rolled off him. I began to pound on the fatman's face like a bongo drum till I felt the pain of a pool stick across my back! I rolled away and fought to my feet as the fatman's crackwhore continued to beat me like I owed her money! The third wack was her last as I grabbed the cue and kicked the bitch in the camel toe! The slut howled and dropped to the floor holding her injured cooter! It was about this time when the local county mounties arrived and slammed me up against the wall. In the end, Lee got a black eye and three cracked ribs.

I got a split lip, cracked tooth, goose egg on my head and broken finger. *"Just like the old days right bro!"* Lee grinned as the cops left with the bikers in cuffs.

"You dumb bastard..you couldn't hit the ground if you fell twice!"

I growled at him. *"Seeing you in a fight is like watching a piss ant pull a freight train!"* I continued to bark at him. *"I knew you'd have my back Doc"* Lee grinned. *"I have come to the conclusion Lee, that you are not the smartest peanut in the turd!!"* I grumbled as I left to find a couple of ice packs, lick my wounds and try to stay the fuck out of trouble.

Tylenol and Tiger Balm the breakfast of Champions!

Identification is very important in bouncing, I can't stress this point enough. In a fight it is imperative that people see and identify you as security. I've seen more security get hurt because the fighting party thought the bouncer was just another guy looking for a piece of the action.

Let some punk bouncing in an Ed Hardy T-shirt grab me. Son, I will be on his ass like a bad rash! I argue this point with employers all the time about security shirts. The shirts should have SECURITY written in plain sight on both back and front. Now you see the importance of a bright colored security shirt. I'm not saying its got to be fuckin glow in the dark shit brindle, but a color that can be easily seen and identified by both the patrons and fellow security team members. Whether we like it or not, we have to dress for the trade. We need to wear clothes that will not be a disadvantage in a fight. A bouncer should always carry his own First-aid kit. This is really important. At most places I've worked the First-aid kits are incomplete. They have First-aid kits all right, but they are usually half empty! First-aid kits should be checked each time the fire extinguishers are checked. And that is every night before your shift!

I carry my own personal Cooler's First-Aid kit. It's a locking metal First-aid kit, with my name printed on the outside. It contains all the usual stuff, and a quick reference medical book.

I also include extra gauze, Band-Aids, extra Ibuprofen, Rolaids, lip balm, a large bag of sore throat lozenges, foam ear plugs, latex gloves, wet wipes and a small mini-mag flashlight with extra batteries.

Always keep your kit locked or it will get raided. Make sure that you have quick access to it at all times. A bouncer should carry, on his belt, a small Mini Mag-lite to help check ID's, for finding lost things on the floor, or walking employee's to their cars. Today I carry a small flashlight that has not only LED lights, but build-in UV light and Red Laser. I call it my Darth Holiday Lightsabre.

Some clubs need armed security to make night money drops, do courier work, etc. If you are doing this, keep your armed security and your bouncing separate. The jobs are totally different. Keep it that way! Personal armed security is serious business on a entirely different level.

I have been a professional bodyguard licensed with SEAL Bodyguard International since 1993. If you're going to do armed security or bodyguard work, go to a reputable school, get trained and certified. Your life and the life of your client depends on it. If you're going to carry a firearm outside the club be legal. Take a firearms proficiency course from a reputable organization, the local police can advise you. Then apply and get a concealed weapons permit, obey the law and practice good gun sense.

A bouncer is a person in the limelight. He meets a lot of people, some like him and some don't. The ones that don't will either let it go or fuck with you when the opportunity presents itself. If they can't get at you they'll get at something that belongs to you, like your vehicle.

Going to your car after a hard night at work and finding a busted windshield and four slashed tires really sucks. If you don't have secured parking, it's best to park down the street in a residential area if possible, or at a business that stays open late as you do, like a 24-hour gas station, truckstop or coffee shop. If you park in front of someone's house be polite. Wearing your work shirt, ask the resident of the house if you may park there. Why? Most people will be impressed by your common courtesy and will most likely keep an eye on your vehicle for you. Now when you leave the club, it gives the impression that you live near the club. Never leave personal information in your car where people can read it though the windows. I see this a lot. You got these morons hanging their picture ID work badges on their rear-view mirrors for every fuckin criminal and sex offender to see! That's about as dumb as lighting a match in a room full of Ass-Gas! Never give out personal information about yourself or the club to people you don't personally know. An easy way to get at a bouncer is to have a chick with a great set of attitudes invite him out for a drink, and into an ambush. Expect the expected! Now we get to a subject that has to be touched upon. In this business there are always going to be fights, some verbal and some physical. Like I tell people at my club, "They didn't hire me here for my extremely good looks." The job of a bouncer is to prevent a verbal argument from going physical. Sometimes we can stop it verbally but sometimes we have to get physical, using the 'necessary force' needed to stop the unruly person or persons. There is a big difference between 'necessary' and 'over-excessive' force. I strongly suggest you get it right the first time unless you like being arrested for assault and battery.

I always say "We are in the Tuggin' & Pullin' business.." So a bouncer must be able to defend himself and protect his fellow employees, as well as the patrons in his club. Team work is always the best way, but sometimes it's just you and the other person or persons - man to man and hand to hand. Many people ask me what the best art is for a bouncer. I would have to say that a combination of boxing and wrestling is best in a bar full of people. I have been boxing since I was 10 years old. My uncle Tommy Hudson was a Golden Gloves champion in Canada in 1947. My cousins and I all boxed for Bob Edgett's Boys Club. I was a boxing coach at the South Side Boxing Legion in Alberta Canada in 1984 and trained quite a few military personnel who joined the gym. Boxing has been a prerequisite for Military hand-to-hand combat in the Canadian Armed Forces since World War I. It's an easy art to learn and excellent for close combat where there is restricted space like a crowded bar. Over the years and with the introductions of HD-digital security cameras, punching someone on security camera looks BAD!! To most court judges, it looks REALLY Fuckin' BAD!! So that is why today I lean more toward Freestyle Wrestling Techniques. This is the same style of wrestling taught in high school and colleges around the country. Wrestling and grappling techniques are excellent to be able to handle an opponent that needs to be restrained until he calms down or other bouncers arrive to help remove him. Bottom-line is I'm not saying you let some guy stomp a mud hole dry in your ass! All I am saying is maintain control of the situation. Self-control and a cool head always prevails. Remember your ABC's of Bouncing.

Weight training is excellent for building strength and power. I have weight-trained for years and still do at 52 years old. I have never used anabolic steroids. I was too scared of needles and worse, ending up with a small dick! Every man makes his own choices but I believe if you train hard and eat right you'll achieve your personal fitness goal. Nowadays, the muscle building supplements are so good, who needs to chance permanent liver damage! Muscles are like parts on a drag bike, if they aren't making horsepower, they're dead weight. I train for power, low reps and heavy weight. I use the treadmill and bike to build endurance. If two guys in a fight are evenly skilled, it will come down to the person who has the stamina to go the distance. In any type of fighting match you can see the importance of conditioning and endurance as the fight carries into the later rounds. Remember, the bigger the muscles, the more energy and oxygen it takes to move them. I've seen a lot of big men with Lamborghini bodies and Volkswagen engines.

Roid Boys are like sailboats -> Out of wind – Out of Power!

Weight training builds strength.

- Flexibility builds speed.
- Repetition builds reflexes.
- Practice builds technique.
- Technique balances the scales of strength and speed to generate power.

Bottom line is, sooner or later you're going to be involved in a fight. My advice to you is, be prepared.

Like I tell my boys *"Don't think of it as a fight...think of it as job security!"*

In some clubs there are fights every night, for example, in clubs that cater to a younger crowd, ages ranging from eighteen to their early twenties. Most of these kids are punks, but don't underestimate them. In the past ten years with the rise of street gangs, these little bastards will shank you or put a cap in your ass faster than you can blink an eye. Respect is everything, even if the person is younger than you. Always talk to him or her with respect. I use to specialize in clubs that dealt with 1%ER's**. Over the years I developed an understanding of their laws and codes. I was what you would call a diplomat when it comes to dealing with these potentially dangerous people. I have been to a lot of club houses and talked to club presidents about business pertaining to the bar, on behalf of the bar owners. Let me hit you with some knowledge bro.. I've read and heard a shit load of crap about how bouncers have taken on gangs and kicked their asses. I assure you these people have been watching too many Jean-Claude Van Damme movies. If a gang puts a bounty on your head you got two choices :

    1) Get your fuckin' ass on the next stage outta Dodge and hope they don't find you.
    2) Find someone who can talk on your behalf to the club's president to see if the problem can be rectified and set your ass to praying!

  ** 1%ER – A member of an Outlaw Motorcycle Club (Hells Angels, Outlaws) etc.

Because I don't care if you're the Grand Master of Jack Shit, bottom line is you are a dead S.O.B. End of story. Did you know that the worst ass kicking I ever got was from four motorcycle gang members. It was Memphis, Tennessee in the winter of 1996. I was working with a brother called Andy at a Biker bar on Macon. The story goes like this.. I was watching this young guy playing pool with a couple of Outlaw Motorcycle gang members. There were two prospects and two full patch holders. The kid was winning and the probates were getting pissed off. The kid said he had to go and left out the front door. Two prospects followed him as the two other full members went out the back door. I told Andy to call the law because I knew shit was about to go down. I ran out the front door to see the kid on the ground and the gang member's boot fuckin' him.

One of the bastard's was swinging a short piece of heavy trucker chain.

I heard a siren and saw a police crusier's lights in the distance so I made my move. The probate who had the chain got a forty yard field goal kick in the balls, from behind, that dropped him like a sack of dirt! I jumped past him and nailed the second probate with a sucker punch behind the right ear that sent him to the concrete. I pushed aside a full patch holder as I shot in to grab the kid by the jacket and started to drag him toward the cruiser that just pulled in. Now the plan was working slicker that an ass crack full of bacon fat till it hit one small problem..the cop that pulled up wasn't really a cop but some old bastard with the Citizen Patrol! It's a well known fact among cat haters that a cat always blinks when you hit it on the head with a ball peen hammer and yes, I knew I was fucked.

I fell on top of the kid that was knocked out and tried to cover up as two patch holders joined by one pissed off prospect with sore balls and a three foot trucker chain took to beating the ever-living dog shit out of me. The last thing I heard was police sirens. When I gained consciousness, I was lying on an ambulance gurney. My right eye was swollen shut and when I turned my head to the left, my nose hit my shoulder. They had fractured my cheekbone, broke my collarbone, dislocated my left shoulder and broke six ribs. But I guess I got off lucky. The kid lost an eye, hearing in his left ear and got a fractured skull. The gangmembers fucked off soon as the real police show up. A thirty second stompin' feels like a lifetime when your on the receiving end. But the boss took care of me and my medical bills. The old boss man let me rest up and later I checked ID's till I got my clavicle brace off. You know the cops told me I saved that kid's life. But the kid's family never said shit to me. Like they say "When I do right no one remembers....when I do wrong no one forgets." This is why I say watch your ass around 1% bikers!

You get a lot of threats in this business but a smart bouncer can usually tell when it's just the liquor talking, or when it's to be taken seriously. My Mom used to say, *"A drunk man's words are a sober man's thoughts."* As for Jean-Claude Van Damme, he can tell you first hand what it's like to mouth off in a bar to a 1%ER and get his ass kicked. In short, the way to handle these people is to let the cooler do the talking and follow his instructions to a tee. In Memphis in 1997, I had a problem with a 1% motorcycle club selling drugs in the strip club where I was working. Their ol' ladies were working and dealing at the same time. The owner asked me to talk to the club president to see if I could do something about it. I knew the president, so I went to the clubhouse.

A member met me at the front gate and took my gun, then led me to the president sitting in the backyard. I sat in the chair beside him and the prospect handed him my nickle plated Desert Eagle .50 cal. The 'Doc Holiday' engraved on the side in old English flashed in the sunlight.

"So you're still carrying this fuckin' cannon, Doc" he said. He laid down my pistol and showed me his. *"I'll stick to my 45 Colt Commander. Either way, one shot and a motherfucker's history."*

"We have a problem that needs to be rectified so we can continue to enjoy a lucrative business relationship" I said.

"God dammit, Holiday. Will you fucking speak plain English!"

I ran down the whole thing to him, concluding with the fact that if the cops get involved we all lose big. He said he'd think about it. Then, without warning, he chambered a round in his 45 and pointed it in my face.

"You fuck with me Doc, and I'll kill your ass." He knew he had me cold.

IVAN 'DOC' HOLIDAY

"*My grand daddy once told me, the man holdin' the gun is the man that does all the talkin*" I said. Bone grinned. I knew I was holding a deadman's hand and the devil was knockin'. "*You know Bone*" I took a deep breath. "*If I had a dollar for every son of a bitch that stuck a gun in my face, I'd be a fucking millionaire.*" My eyes looked into his as I talked through clenched teeth. "*If you feel that I've disrespected you, then drop that fuckin' hammer and go to work!*" Bone laughed as he pulled the gun away. "*That's what I like about you Doc. You got balls big enough to carry in a dump truck*" He handed me my .50 Desert Eagle. "*Not really,*" I said, putting the Eagle back in my shoulder holster. "*The way I see it, if you shot me, you'd have a fuck of a time explaining it to the FBI or whoever in the fuck that is in the white van across the street. How many fuckin' cable companies do you know that work on Sunday!*"

4

"The only mistake in life is the lesson not learned"
- Einstein

Laws change from state to state and country to country. If I wrote down every one I would have a 5,000-page book. I just took the most important ones that pertain mainly to bouncing and listed them in this book in layman's terms, so they are easier to understand. If you're in doubt, ask the owner or manager of your club. He should know the liquor laws that govern his state, or ask a police officer next time one comes into the bar.

The police are a bouncer's heavy artillery. They are always ready to help security if called upon. Always treat police officers with respect and offer them a nonalcoholic drink when they stop by. They are a bouncer's best backup when shit gets totally out of control. But I'll give you a little bit of my vast knowledge. You ever wonder why police officers get pissed off when they are called to a club or bar to arrest some asshole you just punched out. Because not only does the officer have to do a shitload of paperwork on the offender but the police officer has to drag his sorry ass to the emergency room and sit there till some doctor has time to examine him. Even for a fucking scratch, this police officer has to sit for sometimes up to four hours to get this guy cleared by a doctor. So as a rule of thumb, try to handle your trouble in-house and avoid calling the police unless it's absolutely necessary. Local PD will appreciate it and so will your boss.

Three people that can shut a club down faster than shit are:

1. Liquor Control
2. The Fire Marshall
3. Health Department

A 'MINOR' is a person too young to drink alcoholic beverages. The age limit is usually Twenty-one years and older to drink in a bar. Some bars allow minors over the age of Eighteen in their bar but they can only have nonalcoholic drinks and have to wear colored wristbands. Some just go old school and used a large black marker to make a big 'X' on the back of the hand. Personally, this is what I call a bar looking to lose their liquor license and a bouncer's nightmare! We're bouncers not baby sitters, but if a club is going to do this they need to keep a good eye on the under aged patrons. A person must have a valid picture ID to drink in a bar. If you suspect a person is not of legal age, and they do not have a proper ID, they must leave the property.

The four acceptable picture Identifications are:

1. Valid state issued Identification
2. Valid state drivers license
3. Passport
4. Military Identification

Minors can kill a club! Watch for fake ID's or Minors using other older friends ID's – that's the big trend today. With the introduction of UV holograms, high end fakes are hard to get or find. But the ID of an older sister who is Twenty-one is a perfect fake for the younger sibling. Beware of the INTERNATIONAL DRIVERS LICENSE - there is no such thing.. its fake. Plus if you got a person from another country...only way their ass got in the country is with a PASSPORT...so lets see it!!

When a person shows you an ID in a wallet, have the person to take it out of the wallet so you can inspect it. If you are in doubt of an ID ask the person what their middle name is and their date of birth, If you can't read it don't accept it. Over the years I have learned that HEIGHT is a dead giveaway!! Most minors never check height on the ID's.

The fact of the matter is, if a person had a valid ID, and got busted by the police for it being fake, as long as the club is making a 'VALID' attempt to check ID's at the door, they will not lose their liquor license or get fined. We are not expected to catch every fake ID, just to do our best. ID machines that scan for fakes, are a TOTAL fuckin' waste of time and money! Always have been. Little Ms. Seventeen-N-Stacked in a miniskirt and six inch stilettos, hands the bouncer her older sister's ID. Shithead checks out her 36C's, swipes the driver's license and it reads good. End result, Babydoll gets the green light and parties her little minor ass off.

Fuckin' Garbage! No machine can replace an experienced bouncer with a good set of eyes and proper training. When I work at a club, I hold a bouncer team meeting ½ hour before shift. Be late and not call, your ass is fired! Call late more than three times, your ass is fired! This meeting is to bring the team up to speed on management news, the evening events, check equipment and organize positions. You don't see a fucking football team arriving two minutes before kickoff!! Sometimes I like to bring in the Liquor Control people to give a talk on IDs and the law. They have excellent staff for this and you get a chance to see a number of different fake IDs firsthand. It's also good public relations for the bar. It lets the Liquor Control people see that the club takes their security seriously.

A bar or club is private property and reserves the right to serve or not serve alcohol to any person or persons. Management also has the right to have any person or persons asked to leave their place of business without any explanation or reason.

When it comes to weapons in a bar, FIREARMS EXCLUDED, it is at the discretion of the owner or manager of your club.

In a place that serves the public alcoholic beverages such as a bar or nightclub, the only people that can carry a firearm on their person are:

1. The owner of the establishment.
2. Law enforcement officers, on or off duty. (Reason: a police officer is considered on duty 24 hours.)
3. Any agent of Law Enforcement, on or off duty (Example: FBI, Coastguard, ATF, Sheriff, Military Police).

No employee can carry a firearm in a bar, not even the manager; the owner or owners, only!

A person who has a concealed weapons permit cannot carry a firearm in a bar. This includes bodyguards, private investigators, and security guards unless they are on duty, in uniform and have business in the club. This must be cleared with management. If a bouncer suspects a person in civilian clothes to be carrying a concealed firearm, he has the right to ask that person to produce a law enforcement identification. But, be careful. Any nut can get a fake badge and ID out of a mail-order magazine these days.

Just because we are bouncers, doesn't mean we are exempt from the law. A bouncer is held accountable for his actions, just as a police officer is for his. The club is held responsible for your actions as well. If you unjustly hurt someone and are guilty of it, they will sue the club and you personally. I had a friend about twenty years ago who was a bouncer. In self-defense punched a punk kid. The kid hit his head causing some kind of brain damage or so they said. Mack quit bouncing over the incident. The kid's father was a wealthy businessman and had connections. The bar's insurance paid out. They sued Mack but he had nothing. He left the state that year. He came in to a small inheritance later on down the road, got married, bought a new house and opened a small Harley repair shop.

Five years later the kid's father brought Mack back into civil court. Mack lost his shop and the house which was considered part of the business. A bouncer's best defense is to know the Rights and Laws that govern his job.

ASSAULT

Any willful attempt to threaten to inflict injury upon the person of another, when coupled with an apparent present ability so to do, and any intentional display of force such as would give the victim reason to fear or expect bodily harm, constitutes an assault. An assault may be committed without actually touching, or striking, or doing bodily harm, to the person of another. Verbal threats to cause bodily harm directed toward a person is considered assault.

ASSAULT AND BATTERY

Any unlawful touching of another which is without justification or excuse. To assault a person using any form of physical contact.

ASSAULT WITH A DANGEROUS OR DEADLY WEAPON

An unlawful attempt to offer to do bodily harm without justification or excuse by use of any instrument calculated to do harm or cause death.

AGGRAVATED ASSAULT

Any attempt to cause serious bodily injury to another or causes such injuries, with or without a dangerous or deadly weapon with the intention of committing some additional crime; example: a mugging, where the person is physically attacked and robbed.

Doc's Scrapbook
Three Decades of Working the Door

Son Caine and me - Roadhog Saloon, Laconia, NH 2000

IVAN 'DOC' HOLIDAY

Caine & Dad – On location at our Reality TV shoot - 2011

THE BOUNCER'S BIBLE

Caine and sister Rianna

Three Generations - Grandfather Yvon, Grandson Caine and father Ivan

IVAN 'DOC' HOLIDAY

Doc and wife Shirley

THE BOUNCER'S BIBLE

The Legend

Shirley and Doc at Froggy's Saloon 1999

IVAN 'DOC' HOLIDAY

My first boxing trophy at age 12

The Legend on the Door

My 2010 UK Tour

IVAN 'DOC' HOLIDAY

Doc & Rockin' Mel Cardonell – Sturgis Biker Rally, South Dakota, 1999

Rockin' Mel and Crusher – Sturgis Biker Rally, South Dakota, 1998

It get's a little boring at the laundry mat

THE BOUNCER'S BIBLE

The Lynyrd Skynyrd boys –
(Top) Freebird Bob Burns, (Bottom) Jimmy Van Zant

IVAN 'DOC' HOLIDAY

Old School Bouncers –
(Top) Dougie Foo-Foo , Sleazy Larry, Tony The Butler

The Champ – Chet Ballenger

My Riverside Cafe Crew – Chris, Nova, Doc and Ben

THE BOUNCER'S BIBLE

Band security for the Queen of the Blues – Debbie Davis

IVAN 'DOC' HOLIDAY

David & Ellen Lane sponsors of the Riverside Cafe Nascar Truck

THE BOUNCER'S BIBLE

Riverside Cafe sponsored NASCAR
(Driver) Aric Almirola & David Lane

IVAN 'DOC' HOLIDAY

Riverside Cafe – Band Security for CMT star Jake Owen

Doc & Old Sam Crow my 1978 Harley Shovelhead – July 2010

Old school biker

In Iraq training US soldiers in heavy tactical equipment. Sept – Nov 2008

In Iraq with the 225 and 175 Stryker Brigade.

IVAN 'DOC' HOLIDAY

Doc in the bone-yard with one of Saddam Hussein tanks - Taji, Iraq

THE BOUNCER'S BIBLE

R & R on the SS ROADHOUSE - my 1972 Irwin 32 Classic sailboat

IVAN 'DOC' HOLIDAY

Gone but never forgotten

Big Craig (RIP)

Russel The Love Muscle (RIP)

THE BOUNCER'S BIBLE

Rockin' Mel with wife Dorrine (RIP)

IVAN 'DOC' HOLIDAY

Uncle Tommy on old Sam Crow 1999 (RIP)

THE BOUNCER'S BIBLE

Cornelius 'CP' Scully (RIP)

5

"For fools rush in where angels fear to tread."

- A. Pope

There are many different types of places that serve the drinking public alcohol and entertainment:

- biker bars
- after hour clubs
- bottle clubs
- private clubs
- night clubs
- casinos
- taverns and pubs
- dance halls and discos
- strip joints
- roadhouses
- saloons
- lounges
- country bars
- rock and blues bars
- sport bars
- Concerts and Special Events

The people who frequent these places are as different as the establishments themselves. The type of music played in a bar is not as important as the people that go there but it does dictate the personality of patron that frequent that club.

I think the hardest bars to work in are strip clubs, reason being you get shitty shifts like 9 p.m. to 6 a.m. You've got every drunk person in the city coming in after the regular bars close. If you think you're going to watch the girls, forget it! It's parking lot duty and front door detail for the new guys. You ever tried to empty bar trash dressed in a tuxedo? Don't bullshit me Slim, you can't even drink a cup of coffee without a fucking bib!

Tips are usually given to the house mother, the manager (who is probably the only dick getting any in the fuckin' place) and the faggot DJ, because these broads really believe he's making them money! The *doorman gets to carry their bag to their vehicle for a smile and a "fuck you very much." Some girls do appreciate the bouncer and tip him, but it's usually the head bouncer that gets the cheese.

I had this eighteen year old bitch in Memphis who made a grand in one evening because I recommended her to a wealthy business man and set up the meeting. She tipped me ten fucking dollars!

If you are wondering why the dancers' husbands hang around most of the time, it's to make sure their ol' ladies are working and not fuckin' off in the bathroom doing blow*. In most cases, the ol' man is just a fuckin' loser who sits at home all day getting stoned and watching Jerry Springer.

To top it off, here are girls knocking down a hundred grand plus per year on the average and most of them don't have enough money at the start of the night to buy a pack of cigarettes.

IVAN 'DOC' HOLIDAY

Doorman – A bouncer who is checking ID's at the entrance to a club.

Blow – Cocaine, All-American drug, Aunt Nora, Barbs, Coke, Dream, Foo-foo dust, Her, King's habit, Peruvian lady, Snow, Stardust, Witch and Zip.

After a while the regular girls start having their menstrual periods at the same time of the month and, look out for trying to keep twenty or more dancers with PMS under control! They like to drink and party, usually causing more trouble than the patrons and will fight with another dancer in a heartbeat over a big money customer. Most dancers have a love for two things, drugs and money. The ones that prefer to dig their gold with a fuckin' backhoe, are strictly into sugar daddy's that can supply their needs. Ironically, most have some worthless piece of shit for a husband or boyfriend. Stripper's are true asshole magnets. They start out smoking hot but usually end up struggling to make ends meet with a kid or two and some loser for a husband. If the management finds out a bouncer is screwing a dancer, his job is on the line and usually short term. Reason being if you and your sweet-piece have a falling out, management always sides with the girls. End result, your ass is going to be looking for work elsewhere. Like I said before, ' *Grizzly bear don't shit where he eats*'.

VIP area's are the biggest pain in the ass in strip clubs. If your the sucker stuck at the VIP entrance, you fuckin' better be half accountant and half pimp! You have to keep track of how many songs played, how many private dances the girls have done, how much they owe the house on a per dance bases. Strippers are not angel's or math teachers, so the money count is all on you! All this and you still have to watch a multi-screen security CCTV monitor to make sure the girl's are grinding and not humping! Let me tell you bro, jackin' the shit of some two pump chump who just nutted all over his hands is a nasty motherfucker! End result, you got a dancer screaming because the dude just blew all over her and you got this wasted nutsack trying to tell her and you, he's sorry!

Then you have to get the money and drag Mr. Blueballs out of the club without him putting his filthy paws on your Tux!! Ahh..the good old day!

Way I see it when it comes to bouncers and strippers, if you want to take the chance of having your heart ripped out through your ass, just get in a serious relationship with a tittydancer. I know all about it brother, I was married to one!

An after-hours bar or bottle club would be my second choice for a shitty place to work. Most of these bars are shit holes, where they sweep eyeballs and teeth off the floor at closing time.

Lets stop here for a moment and reflect on what you have learned so far. I think this is a good time for a field trip, bro. We are going on a journey to a high class New York strip club called 'Scores' back in 1998. The bouncer's name is Steve 'Sonny Coats' Hart and this is his story.

I wasn't there the night of the murders. I didn't see the Albanian hitman reach into his jacket, draw his gun, and blow away two of my friends. But while working at Scores, I've seen plenty of crazy shit. I watched a Magazine executive drop $27,000 in a single night trying to get some extracurricular action from two gorgeous strippers. I've seen big name celebrities drool over the dancers- yeah, I'm talking about you George Clooney. I've seen chair-throwing barroom brawls and mountains of silicone and a small army of well-dressed wiseguys. But one thing that still haunts me is Ricky. See, Ricky had a chippy. When you spend as much time in a strip club as I have, you see this all the time: It's an addiction to a dancer. One dancer. In this case, Maria, a sloe-eyed Hispanic brunette with ready breasts and swivel hips.

For 10 weeks running, Ricky, a hot shot in the clothing business, stuffed an endless stream of twenties into her garters for lap dances and whispered promises. One night Ricky came up to me, and I could tell he had something on his mind.

"You know, Sonny," he said, " I've spent $ 40,000 on this girl and I haven't even gotten a fuckin' blow job." Now I genuinely liked Ricky, and seeing him throw his money away made me queasy. I wanted to let him in on the truth : that strippers were a fantasy, to be seen but not touched and never, ever taken home. But telling the truth wasn't so easy. After all , I was part of the fantasy. Since 1994, I've worked as a bouncer at Scores, a topless club in New York City. When I started, it wasn't just another two-bit strip club, it was 'the' strip club. This is where Nicolas Cage, Madonna, Ethan Hawke, Mark Wahlberg, and that cheap bastard George Clooney came to party. This is where Demi Moore researched her role for Striptease. Dennis Rodman was a regular; so were Howard Stern and Mickey Rourke.

The Wall Street guys who were pulling down $15 million a year? They were here, too, puffing on Cubans while sitting on the club's plush couches, drinking $100 shots, and throwing fistfuls of cash at the strippers for lap dances and maybe a quickpeek beneath the G-string. Even the mob guys, who could go anywhere and do anything, made Scores their home.

The place was a circus: In one corner, celebrities might be trading punches; in another, a dancer could be giving a guy a hand job. You never knew what was going to happen - that's why the customers kept coming. If you were rich and in New York, you came to Scores. You came for the privilege of having the world's *most beautiful girls take their clothes off for you. You came to Scores for the fantasy.*

I got my job at Scores the old fashioned way: I knew someone. I'd just gotten out of the joint for selling steroids, and was flat fucking broke. I was concentrating on my bodybuilding and I was making a little money as a personal trainer, but I needed a job to support my six-year-old son. There was no way in hell I was going to let him down. Scores offered me a part-time gig, and I accepted it on the spot.

Scores wasn't the first club I'd worked for. At Show World, a sex club in Times Square, I handed out coins so guys could jerk off in peepshow cubicles. For a few bucks I'd turn my back so Joe Schmo could sneak a dancer into a compartment. I also worked at Studio 54. I know what your thinking: Andy Warhol, Liza Minnelli, enough coke to build Frosty the Snowman. It wasn't like that. During the late 80's the Studio was on its last legs. The place was serving soda, and 15-year-olds were offering to blow me just to get in. And no, I didn't. If they were of age, well, that was a different story. What can I say? It was a stressful job.

But Scores was something else. It had the feel of a Vegas casino: no clocks, no windows to let early morning sun in, and a register that never stopped ringing. Dance music pumped as beautiful women disrobed everywhere. On a Saturday night, about 125 dancers were on duty and it looked like a Roman orgy . . . except that all the guys had their clothes on and none of them were particularly Roman. The talent was spectacular. Some of these girls had been Baywatch extras or in Penthouse and I was working with them, side by side-or closer. I remember taking a dinner break on one of my first nights and having this stripper's ass come two inches from my linguine.

But I couldn't let my johnson get the best of me. I had a job to do; my son was counting on me. My first assignment was to stand in the lobby and ask patrons to check their coats. Actually, it was more of an order than a request. See, anyone who doesn't check their coat and pay the three-dollar fee is simply not admitted to Scores. Consider it an additional admission charge. Once in a while if some guy started to bitch and moan, I'd tell him to hit the street. You get the picture: Everyone had to check their coat. After about six months, management put me on full-time. I guess they liked the way I convinced patrons to check their coats. Of course, Demi never had to check her coat. She could do anything she damm well pleased. Scores treated all its celebrity guests like royalty, and the stars liked it that way. But the celebs didn't always return the favor. One night I did George Clooney the courtesy of telling him that a herd of paparazzi was outside. The guy practically shit a stethoscope; Being seen at a strip club could ruin his pretty-boy image. So I told him I'd sneak him out the back door . . . and he handed me $20. Now, that's a nice tip for a plumber from Brooklyn, but for Mr. $100,000 an Episode, it's chump change. So I tipped off my buddy James, a newspaper photographer. He drove right over to the club and shot tightwad George with a zoom lens as he strolled casually out the back. Guess who made the paper next day.

Clooney wasn't the only star who wanted his visits to Scores a secret. "We weren't here, " I remember two star players from the Indiana Pacers whispering to me one night. They were sitting in the President's Club Room, a sort of club-within-a-club where, on occasion, dancers violated house rules by placing a napkin over a customer's lap, then giving him a hand job.

To avoid attention, Howard Stern and his snickering cronies came to the club during off-hours. I know a certain big-name sportscaster - no, not Marv - who spent 10 days straight getting trashed at the club in the company of a $10,000-a-week call girl.

One exception to the I-wasn't-here rule was Dennis Rodman. Whenever he came to the club, I was assigned to sit with him as he ate dinner and make sure no one hassled him for his autograph. Of course, I was the first one to hit him up. But it was for my son. (no really.) Dennis was always well behaved, a perfect gentleman, and he tipped me $100 just for sitting there. Of course, if he tipped me a $150, I wouldn't be telling you the rumor that a stripper named Peaches knew first hand why Dennis is called the Worm.

One celebrity who wishes he'd never shown his fat Belgian face at Scores is Jean-Claude Van Damme. He was checking out the action one night, a few tables away from a guy named Chuck Zito. Zito's a Hells Angel and a successful actor; He's on that prison TV show 'OZ'. He's also a friend of the club. Everything's cool until Van Damme tells a bouncer nicknamed Frankie Cannoli that "Zito has no heart. He's a punk" and Cannoli repeats the crack to Chuck. A few minutes later, when Van Damme pulls his face out of Peaches' crotch, Chuck is standing right there and simply asks, "Did you call me a punk and say I had no heart?" Van Damme was silent, but he slowly removed his wire-rimmed glasses and slides them into his shirt pocket. If you went to Princeton, taking off your glasses means you finished reading a book. For street guys, it means you're ready to rumble. Chuck didn't wait to see what would happen next: He punched Van Damme in the head so fast that the Muscles from Brussels never saw it coming.

Cannoli, myself, and a few other bouncers jumped in and held Chuck back as the Hard Target cowered on the floor. Then I asked Van Damme to leave; he was most obliging. But of all the spoiled celebrity brats who came to Scores, the biggest bonehead had to be Michael Moore, the former heavyweight champ of the world. Late one night he strolls into the club with a few friends and demands dinner. When someone tells him the kitchen is closed, Moore starts raging and storms into the kitchen. To do what, I don't know. I'm thinking about handing him a frying pan and some meat and telling him to make it himself.

Our head of security, Willie Marshall, has other ideas. Willie's the toughest guy ever to set foot in Scores. He was a corrections officer; now he was moonlighting as a strong-arm for the mob. So Willie confronts the boxer and tells him to "get the fuck out of the kitchen." Moore doesn't take to kindly to those words, and the two square off. I'm standing five feet away from Willie, trying to figure out if Moore's buddies are carrying guns. Everyone's on edge, but I'm a pro and play it cool. For 30 long seconds, nobody says a word. Finally, Moore shakes his head, as if to say "you ain't worth it," and leaves the club, never turning his back on Willie.

It was a Sunday night and this guy named Sammy was drinking at the bar. I'd seen Sammy at the club before, hanging with his mob buddies, dropping big bills. Tonight, though, none of his pals are around, and he's drinking alone. He invites me to join him. We're shooting the shit for a while-he tells me I look like Mark Messier. fuck, I'm thinking, I must be going bald. Then, out of nowhere, he asks who I'm with. What he's really asking me is, am I connected to the mob?

I wasn't quite sure what to say. The wiseguys who frequented the club liked me; they knew I was committed to my son and they respected that. When I greeted them at the front door, they always shook my hand and kissed me on the cheek. They started calling me Sonny Coats, and the name stuck, To be honest with you, I liked the goodfellas. I admired their world of respect and honor, the way kept their word and took care of business. And there was a lot to be said about their lifestyle: all that cash, all that power. Was Sammy just curious . . . or was he making me an offer? Either way, I had to think about it. You never want to say the wrong thing to a wiseguy. "For now," I told him, "I'm with the club. I work under Willie." He nodded and smiled. Scores was crawling with mob guys. There were plenty of nights when the place looked like open casting for The Godfather. See, one of the men who owned Scores, Michael

Blutrich, a fat 49-year-old lawyer and "businessman", had an association with the infamous Gambino family from his days in the restaurant business. The way I saw it, Blutrich and the Gambinos struck a deal: The Gambinos made sure that Scores wasn't blown up by a rival family, and Blutrich gave them a cut of the door, parking, and coat check, even let them pick some of the bouncers. In short, they ran the joint. Of course, if Blutrich didn't go along with them, they might blow the place themselves. Yeah, I guess technically you could call it extortion, but that's how business is done in New York City. Like the celebs, the mob guys were treated like gold. In fact, management didn't have metal detectors at the door, because they didn't want to embarrass anyone. Which meant you never knew when a gun was going to be drawn.

(One night after closing, Willie's mob buddies were drinking hard, and one of the guys suddenly reaches over, yanks a lobster out of the tank, pulls out his piece, and shoots it in the freakin' head.)

It didn't take me long to spot the wiseguys. They were the ones in the Armani suits, Rolex watches, and slicked-back hair; they always looked great and they always carried a big roll of bills, a roll that could of paid my son's first year of college. It looked like quite a life. The mob guys were comped and paid for nothing. They'd steal from wealthy assholes like Blutrich, then turn around and lay serious tips on us $500-a-week grunts.

After a year at coat check, I was officially made a bouncer. I was moving up in the world. Scores needed a shitload of bouncers, because its patrons were rich men with massive egos who were used to getting whatever the hell they wanted. Some of my fellow bouncers, like Willie were heavily connected to the goodfellas; others were simply dumb fellas. Johnny Rockhead, for instances, was a little brain-dead. Many nights I'd walk through the dining room and see Rockhead engaging a dancer in a stimulating conversation about all the guys he wanted to beat up.

Another bouncer, Cue Ball, aspired to nothing more in life than to sleep with a Scores stripper. The girls knew this and told him that they might screw him if his bald spot wasn't so big. So for months Cue Ball tried Rogaine, herbs, any fucking thing to grow hair. With hair not growing and the girls not cooperating, Rockhead and Cue Ball turn their efforts to scramming the club. Their plan was foiled with in 24 hours. A lot of guys I know tell me they work with beautiful women, but I can say to you with absolute certainty that during the clubs heyday, my co-workers were some of the best looking women in the world.

Because a good dancer could pull down $2,000 a night, the hottest girls from Florida, Las Vegas, and every bumfucktown in U.S.A. flock to Scores. I'd watch customers happily drop 20, 40, 50 bucks for a three-minute lap dance. Working with girls, I knew the reality. And 11 times out of 10, it wasn't pretty. All the girls had phony names-who the hell names their kid Mahogany? - and all of them had the same story: they were supporting a Nintendo playing deadbeat boyfriend and had come to the club with noble intentions of working for a year, making some quick dough, and buying a home for themselves and their kid. But years later they'd still be taking it off. It was a broken record. Like everyone else at Scores, they became addicted to the money and the fantasy. It was satisfying to have a powerful Wall street V.I.P. drooling over them, dreaming about them; the dancers loved that power. In the dressing room, they were always raggin' on the guys that were paying them, calling them cheap losers. That pissed me off: I mean if you hate stripping so much, why don't you learn to type? To get through a night of dancing, they often loaded up on booze, maybe did a bump of coke. Once a former call girl was so fucked up that she got on the stage wearing two different shoes; another time she passed out and pissed on herself. Management didn't mind that the girls were a little looped. They knew that booze loosened the girls up: maybe it would allow them to brush their nipple against some guy's forehead and he'd blow another 100 bucks on two rounds of drinks.

When I started working at Scores, I pledged to myself that I'd never get involved with a Scores girl-but that was before I was sucked into the party atmosphere. Her name was Milena. She had beautiful olive skin, thick black hair, a rock-hard ass, and drugstore tits, and most important, she needed to get off work early one night.

The two of us made an agreement : I'd talk to the manager on her behalf, and she'd spend a little time with me in the employee's bathroom. Her leg was propped up on the sink, my tuxedo pants kept falling to the urine-soaked floor, and we both could hear the guys in the kitchen cursing in Spanish. Not one of my most romantic moments, but fuck it. I can say I screwed a Scores girl and you can't. The fun and games ended on June 21, 1996. Thursday nights were always crowded, because that's when the Wall Street guys cut loose, but this evening was especially packed. Things didn't feel right: maybe the mood was a little too rowdy, maybe the wannabes were drinking more than usual. Or maybe it was just me. I'd been fasting to prepare for a bodybuilding competition, and I was starting to cramp, so I asked to go home. Jon, a waiter who graduated from a fancy college in Pennsylvania, and Mike who'd grown up in the Bronx, covered the door. It would be tough to find two more different backgrounds, but they were both good kids. At 4 a.m. the club closes. Willie and his girlfriend Lori are hanging out, having a few drinks before locking up. Jon, Mike, a few dancers, and three Albanians reputed to be hit men are there too. Everything's pretty low-key until Jon and one of the Albanians start arm wrestling. Jon beats the guy and then starts laughing. Big mistake. The Albanian lifts Jon up by his shirt. Lori screams, and the Albanian tells her to shut the fuck up. Nobody talks to Willie's girlfriend like that, and Willie instructs Jon and Mike to show the Albanians the door.

IVAN 'DOC' HOLIDAY

As Jon's unlocking the door, according to my friends, one of the Albanians slips his gun from his jacket and, pulls the trigger four times. Jon goes down. Dead. Mike turns to run, but before he can get away, he takes a bullet, too.

Mike's casket was covered by a Miami Dolphins' flower arrangement. His head had been blown off. I was the only club employee to go the burial. After the service, I returned to Scores. It was 15 minutes after my shift started, and one of the owners, a slimeball prick named Lyle Pfeffer, had the nerve to ask why I was late. That night everyone pretended like nothing happened. But it was the beginning of the end. Five months later, federal and state investigators raided the club, looking for evidence against the Gambino crime family. In a nut shell, Blutrich and Pfeffer get caught and agree to help the FBI by working undercover for a lighter sentence. Their undercover sting nails Willie to the wall. And guess what? Willie flipped. Nobody could believe he was a rat. But it was true. The rest is history. Today Michael Blutrich, Lyle Pfeffer, and Willie Marshall are in the federal witness protection program. Scores filed for bankruptcy on October 30, 1998 but remains open and popular.

When I read Sonny Coats' story in *Maxim Magazine*, I thought it was excellent and that it needed to be shared with others in our trade. There is a lesson to be learned here. True, there are some things that I don't agree with but overall I feel that Sonny Coats was a professional and a standup guy. I hope today things are still good for Sonny and his son.

When looking for a bouncing job, dress well and have a good resume with you. Have good solid references that can be easily reached. Letters of recommendation are always good. Nothing pissed me off more then having some swingin' dick give me a resume and then when I call his phone number I get a fuckin' recorder. Then the asshole has the nerve to call me back a week later. End result..your ass is fired before your hired!

When looking at a club or bar for a job, go in on a busy night and just watch. Watch the bar staff and the bouncers. Feel the place out, check out the crowd. What's the atmosphere of the club? Is it rockin', slow, dead? What's the crowd; young, old, half and half? Are the bouncers doing their jobs? Ask yourself this question, *"Would I want these bouncers watching my back?"* Do the bouncers seem over aggressive? Does the club have a reputation for having bad security?

When I work a club I expect my fellow bouncers to give me both barrels, with no hesitation when it's time to rock.

"Never leave a fallen comrade," is a line from the Ranger's Creed of the Special Forces. I have lived by these five words all my life, and I install it in all of my bouncers. I'm proud to be a bouncer and proud to be accepted as the best damm Cooler in the business. I train everyday to be in top condition both mentally and physically.

In the famous words of the Nature Boy, Rick Flair:

"If you want to be the man . . you got to beat the man! Woooo!"

If the club you are checking out seems ok, talk to the bartender when he or she is not busy. Talking to the D.J. is even better, they always have the inside scoop on the bar. When you finally talk to the head bouncer never come off as a guy who can eat lead, shit bullets and piss napalm! Don't try to break his hand when you shake it to show him how strong you are! Be polite and come across as a team player. Never discuss fighting or such related subjects during your interview. Never talk bad about other clubs or club owners. *"If you don't have anything* good to say about somebody, then don't say anything," my uncle Eldred use to say.

He also said, "If you give a dog enough rope it will hang itself and a person's tongue will do the same thing."

When you work, dress accordingly. You don't dress like a fuckin' Walmart cowboy when working at a biker bar. You never want to draw the wrong kind of attention to yourself or try to make any statements. It's not the beach or a fashion show. You want to be a pro..dress like one!

When you are hired, get the necessary important information from your boss. Make sure of your days, hours, and pay scale.

It is very important to make sure you will have medical and dental coverage if you get hurt on the job.

Make sure you understand fully how the manager or the head bouncer wants the show run and try your best to run it his way. Things always look good on the drawing board but most of the time they don't work worth a shit in the club. That's why a bouncer has to be able to handle unseen problems as they arise.

Like I used to tell my friend and ex-boss Jay Allen of the world famous Broken Spoke Saloon, *"That's why you pay me the big bucks!"*

Most important of all is, never hire on to a club or bar where you're in over your head. If it's a major rough bar, and you are inexperienced, or a married guy with a regular day job and a family to feed, do yourself and your family a favor and work somewhere else.

Whenever I hire a new bouncer on I have certain questions I ask: *"Are you a fighter?"*.. *"Are you married?"*, *"Got kids?"*, *"Do you cheat on your wife?"* As a rule of thumb, a married man who is true to his wife makes a good bouncer because he needs the job. He will keep his mind on the job at hand and not on the women in the bar.

If you are a married man and your wife loves you, you're a very lucky man. If you think the grass is greener on the other side of the fence, it's not. I've been working the other side of the fence for thirty years and I've come to learn that the grass is always greener over a septic tank!

When I think of a married bouncer, I think of my friend Rockin' Mel Cardonell. We worked at Froggy's Saloon in Daytona Beach back in the day. Way back in the day! Not only is he still a great bouncer but he is a fine example of a man who loved and respected his wife *Doreen and his family. As a matter of fact, I'm still getting a few pointers from Mel.

God knows I need all the help I can get.

*The wife of my best friend Rockin' Mel Cardonnel passed away in 2009. Doreen was a beautiful person, loving wife and mother. She was loved by all who had the pleasure to know her.

Ex-military make good bouncers once taught the ropes. They follow protocol well and are trained professionals. As a general rule they are good men with the potential to be good bouncers, if they are willing to learn the trade. Never Law Enforcement or Corrections..nuff said. I can't help but think of Crusher when I talk about Rockin' Mel. What a great pair of brothers to back up my shit! Sometimes I would joke and say *"I'd like you to meet the fuckin' Hammer Brothers...Jack & Sledge!"* lol

Rockin' Mel was always the Talk or Rock type bouncer. But Crusher was more the Rock and Talk kind, if you know what I mean. He was an old school hammer and came in mighty handy when it was time to throw down and the odds were not in old Doc's favor. I still remember the time when I was having trouble with this asshole at a biker rally in Sturgis, South Dakota. Crusher was standing just behind my right shoulder, Rockin' Mel on my left. I was having a heated conversation with this rolex rider on a geezer glider. He claimed he got ripped off by one of the beer tub girls. I tried to tell him I would investigate the issue but he just kept getting more and more irate. Of course the accused beer tub girl was no help standing there putting her two cents worth in and calling him a fat bastard. Well Rockin' Mel took the beer tub bitch for a wall to cool off as I was just about to finish talking to this chickenhead. Dude said a final *'Fuck you'* and poked his finger in my face. A large fist the size of an eight pound sledgehammer came over my right shoulder and nailed this fat bastard in the forehead. This shitbag hit the ground like he was struck by lightening! I wheeled to face Crusher with a combination of surprise and anger.

"*Crusher..What da fuck!*" Crusher jumped back with a surprised look on his face. "*Doc..he was makin' a move!*" Crusher replied in his strong New Jersey accent that sounded like baritone Rocky Balboa.

"*Making a move?*" I said glancing at the sack of shit on the ground who's eyes kept rolling back into his head. At this time two smaller men were making a piss poor attempt to get this ass-wipe on to his feet.

"*Wwwhat?*" Crusher opened his arms wide as I put my full attention back on him.

"*Doc..I swear on my mother's grave he was makin' a move!*" a sympathetic Crusher said.

"*Crusher your mother ain't even dead!!*" I shot back.

"*Yo Doc...your like father to me.*" Crusher sucked up.

"*I suppose his ass is dead too..*" I growled.

"*Naaa..he's in Brooklyn!*" Crusher smirked.

"*Your fuckin' killin me...*" I uttered in a low tone.

"*But Doc..*" he blurted out.

I pointed a stern finger in his direction that stopped him cold.

Rockin' Mel returned. He looked at the two small men dragging the semi-conscience fatman outside and then at Crusher.

"*Wwwhat?*" Crusher looked at Rockin' Mel who was now smiling, tight lipped.

"*Yo, he was makin' a fuckin' move...OK!*" Crusher said defensively.

"*I didn't say shit.*" Rockin' Mel replied with a shit-eating grin.

"*Ok Bro, I see how it is...*" Crusher continued *"Your gonna give me that fuckin' D-Esclade-shun bullshit again!"* Crusher grabbed his crotch and shook it, "*I got your fuckin' D-Esclade-shun shit right here!!*" Any Italian wiseguy would have been proud but at this point I had given up all hope and just walked away toward the coffee machine, shaking my head.

I don't think Crusher ever got de-esclation and conflict management.

Hell Crusher was so stubborn and hard headed, he'd bitch about the rope you hung him with! Lol

Just another chapter in the life and times of Roadhouse Doc Holiday.

There is a thing I call my Bouncer Joke. I tell it to every new bouncer that hires on to break the ice and to see if he has a sense of humor. I believe that a good bouncer has to have a sense of humor.

I got the joke from a brother of mine named Gordo in Memphis, Tennessee. Brother Gordo and I worked a wack of stripclub's in Memphis. What I always liked about Gordo was when I was losing a fight, he'd pull them off me and when I was winning a fight ,he'd pull me of them! He was one hell of a bouncer back in the day. When Gordo and another Xtra large brother of mine SS got to bangin' heads, I stayed the fuck out of it. Two men over six foot and over three hundred pounds, I'd have better luck breaking up to two Rhinos going at it in a china shop! I still miss SS, who passed on while back. We rode together and bounced together.

A true Iron Horseman and hardcore 1% brother.

Today Brother Gordo is managing a stripclub in Florida not far from my bar and we usually hookup once a month to smoke a stogie and talk about the good old days.

Anyway, the joke goes like this:

A circus was traveling through the Amazon jungle when all of a sudden they were attacked by a horde of cannibal pygmies.

Everyone in the circus was killed.

That night the pygmies had a large bonfire and were dancing in Conga lines and chanting.

At the center of the camp sat the chief and the witchdoctor on a pile of bones.

The chief turned to the witchdoctor, handed him a bone and said, "Does this clown taste funny to you?"

I love that joke! Fuck you, it's my book and I'll write it anyway I want. Plus you bought it, so just shut up and keep reading!

Do you have any idea what it's like to work a ten hour shift with a bouncer who has no sense of humor and the personality of a rock!

Its just like wiping your ass with a wagon wheel..there just ain't no end to it!

I remember Dean's bouncer joke. He was the Head of Security at the Wildwest in Edmonton, Alberta, Canada in 1990.

He'd ask:

If your Uncle Jack was stuck on his horse . . . would you help your Uncle Jack off his horse? I miss working for that shit head!

I was working a club in Phoenix, Arizona when I saw ten members of a local motorcycle club pull up flying colors. I told the front desk girl that if I touched my ear she was to call the local police to come for a walk through. I tried to talk them into keeping their colors off while in the bar.

"I'm sorry bro, we don't allow colors in the club. Its management's deal and I'm just pass on the message," I told them. They got pissed off and began to threaten me. I touched my ear and told them that I respected them and I was just doing my job. I told them that I would not even try to stop them but that the local police make their rounds about this time and I would hate to see them get arrested. At about this time two police cars showed up. The bikers took off their colors and went in before the officers got to the front door. They later thanked me for the good advice.

Like I said, the bouncer at the door has got to have good eyes and good sense. Bouncing is an art in itself. But then again sometimes you don't see it coming and like Uncle Tommy used to say *'Its the punch you don't see that hits you the hardest!"*

I was working at the Roadhog Saloon at the Laconia Bike Rally back in 2000 with my son Caine. Jerry Shirley & his band Humble Pie were to perform that night. It was around three o'clock in the afternoon and I had five Angel's and their old ladies drop by for a drink. I told the crew that when the HA's are in the house, I work their section alone. I have a good rep with the local chapter vice-president and the last thing I need is one of my boy's to get their ass stomped for being or doing something stupid. I told them if there's a problem I will signal you.

Do not try to help me you'll just make it worse. When you get the signal just call the cops - period. Well all was going good till the band's bass player Rod showed up with a camera. I told him *"Rod keep that camera away from the Angel's or you will be digging it out of your ass!"* Rod nodded *"Ok Doc, I got ya.."* Well ten minutes later Rod Shit-4-Brains is taking a picture of a girl next to the speakers. Hot bitch- Bad idea, it was one of the Angels old ladies!

I saw an Angel get up from the table and head toward Rod. The Angel we'll call "RED" was my height 5'6", well muscled with carrot red hair in a crew-cut and black Buddy Holly style glasses. He grabbed Rob by the jacket collar and slapped the Slash-type hat he liked to wear off his head. Rob covered his camera up in his arms and waited for the next blow. When Red pull back his fist to land a second shot, I jumped in between him and Rob. I felt Red's fist hit the back of my head as I grabbed Rob and jerked him out of Red's grasp. My son Caine and two more security were coming toward me when I threw Rob at them, *"Get this asshole out of here!"*

I barked out the command. My security was dumbfounded as they dragged Rob off. My eyes were still a little glassy from the poke in the back of the head as I turned to see four Angel's rise from the table. I thought

'Nothing like playing Russian roulette with an automatic'. It was Red who got up close and personal in my face and was now nose to nose with me. *"Either your some fuckin' stupid or you got balls that clank!"* he growled through clenched teeth.

"Just getting stupid in my old age." I replied and braced for a smack.

Red studied my face for a few seconds then turned to his brother's at the table and waved for them to sit back down. Fuckin' dodged a bullet big time!

An hour later when the Angels were getting ready to leave, Red came up and said *"No hard feelings.."*

I replied *" Not a problem brother."* Red nodded and the group got on there choppers and left. That's how shit works with 'Real Bikers'.

Later my son Caine asked me *"You ok Dad?"* He looked concerned.

"Just a love tap son." I smiled. *"How about getting your old man a coffee."* Caine grinned *"I got your back..OLDMAN"* and walked away in the direction of the kitchen.

You see sometimes you get these wannabe fucking idiots who form a club and want to play Billy-Badass-Biker. A great example was when I was back working the Roadhog Saloon at the Laconia Bike Rally the next year. Had a great fuckin crew, my son Caine, Danny Funk, Mikey the Mongoose, ThaiBri, Rockin Mel Cardonnel, Red Dog Melvin – Mel's son, Sleazy Larry and Tony the Butler. It went down like this, closing time was three am and we were working everyone out the gate. We had five thousand patrons through the gate that day and we were busier than a Mexican whorehouse on a free taco Friday night! I looked over and noticed a couple of biker's wearing club colors at the main bar talking to a smoking hot piece of ass called Danna. This chick was a fitness instructor by trade with a great set of sugar daddy D-cups and an ass carved out of granite!

Bro this split-tail had a sundress on one day that her ass just devoured!

I mean her ass crack sucked in that dress like a belly-dancers veil caught in a shop vac! Damm..I forgot where I was..oh ya, I went walking up to inform the two bikers that we were closed up. I approached the smaller of the two men and said *"We got to close up partner."* The small guy replied *"don't worry about it..were just pickin' up Danna"*

I looked at Danna who is wearing a micro-bikini top and a pair of air tight black spandex bicycle shorts. I never seen an ass like that in the Tour De France but she could use my face for a seat anytime!

But I guess she had a thing for 2 % bikers and nose candy.

"Well that's fine, but you'll have to wait outside the gate" I replied.

"I think we'll wait right here till she's done" the bigger man stepped up.

"Make sure she's safe" the big man grinned.

"Your a funny guy" I mused. *"But its staff only inside after 3am, I don't make the laws"*. The smaller biker stepped forward and rolled up his right arm sleeve. At this time I noticed Danny the Funkman standing behind the bikers leaning up against Danna's bar. Rockin' Mel and his son Red Dog Melvin were making their way toward my position.

The smaller biker flexed his bicep and pointed at the tattoo in the middle of his chicken wing. *"You see what this says boy!"*

It was a tattoo of the Grim Reaper holding an ace of spades. Under it was the words "DEALERS OF EVIL". I leaned over close and examined the tattoo. Then I pretended to read the inscription "THE – DIDDLERS – OF – EVIL". I stood up and smiled. The little guy was fuckin hot. *"It's Fuckin' DEALERS man!!...DEALERS OF EVIL!!"* he yelled as he pointed a finger at his tattoo. *"Dealers...*

Diddlers...It's all the same shit to me." I replied, staring him down. The look on Danny Funk's face was priceless. He had a shit-eating grin that covered his whole face. I was tired and over this pissing contest. The big man noticed Danny Funk behind him and turned to size him up. It only took a second for the big man to decide it was time for him and his boyfriend to haul ass. Danny took off his security shirt earlier, to help move some beer cases for the manager.

All I need to say about the Funk Man is that he looked like a 5'10" Lou Ferrigno in a white wife-beater. I think you get the fuckin' visual! His broken-toothed '*I'm gonna fuck you up*' grin and eighteen inch arms built from a life time of laying concrete cinder blocks were enough to make any dude sweat. These boys did not want to fuck with the Funk Man Boogy! It's been thirteen years since I last seen my friend Danny Funk. I sure miss him. Last I heard he was up Chicago way with his brother who is a member of the Outlaws MC. I sure miss that boy.

6

"Forgive your enemies, but never forget their names."
- J.F.K

I have always said 'The Door is the Art of Bouncing'. Anyone can work the floor inside the club but the ID Door is a whole different animal.

The man on the door has got to have:

- Good eyes and facial recognition for reading ID's
- have a good professional appearance
- be a people person
- have the ability to read people
- make the call and enforce it
- keep control at the door
- Stop trouble before it enters the club

His good judgment at the door makes it easier for his fellow bouncers to do their job inside the club. That's why I always put my number one man at the door! The boys used to think I was chastising them for putting them at the door. Mr. Gibbs this is for you. As I told Jeffery, I put my best man at the door. My doorman is my front line of defense. Like Dad used to say *"It's easier to keep it out ..than to throw it out!"* Thus, if you are going to have trouble it's best to settle it at the door before it enters the club. The bouncer at the door has to be a real PR man. It is one of the most important positions in the club. He must be able to welcome people to the club, check for proper identification and read a possible bad situation before it enters the club.

Every time I think of PR and supporting the patrons, I think of the times I helped my friend Mrs. Catherine May and her husband George into their handicap SUV. Mrs. May was in a wheelchair and my security team would assist them in getting loaded up and backed out. This makes a person feel good and the job worthwhile. Miss May passed away in 2010.

I enjoyed the chocolate candies she would bring for me and the boys.

I am sure God has a special place for that special lady.

In the world of bouncing you got your great people and then you have the 'Scrotumus Maximus' - Latin for 'worthless nutsack!' A prime example of this is when you get some rich asshole with a silver spoon up his rectum and a Nero complex. It was about three months ago. This older British guy about 350lbs comes up to me and tells me he is being blocked in by a silver truck. He wants it towed immediately. I was not on shift for another two hours but what the fuck. I walk out to parking lot to have a look and here was this silver Ford F-150 'legally parked' next to a Burgundy Maserati. *"I can't tow that truck sir, it's legally parked in the stall."* I said. *"Are you blind man!"* the fat Brit howled *"I can't open my door all the way, so he is obviously parked to close!"* I looked up at him

"Mister how about I back your car out of the parking stall for you."

"This is outrageous!" he yelled *"Fine.. but do be careful,* it's brand new and your salary wouldn't cover the cost of an oil change."

This bastard was so fat, that when he's haul's ass, he has to make two trips! I wondered if they flew his ass here in first class or cargo!

I open the door and hop in the $130,000 Maserati. The goddam thing looks like a 767 jet cockpit inside. The seat was all the way back and laying half way down, the typical fat-man seat position. So I'm lookin' for a start button. Fat Bastard (*from the Austin Powers movie*) is at the passenger window with his face all red yelling instructions. To make a long story short, I found the right buttons and gears. I backed the bitch out, put her in Park then revved her up like a Formula One car in the pit lane!!

9000 RPM – she was one Bad Bitch! I thought Boss Hog was gonna shit brickhouse! When I stepped out of the car the British dude was beet red, leaning on the back fender of the car and loosing his necktie in an attempt to catch his breath. Dude was sweating like a nun in a field of cucumbers! "*This bitch got some serious horsepower fatman!*" I smiled.

"You...you ...MORON!" he croaked!

"Bro, I suggest you either sell the car or hookup with Jenny Craig before someone has to use the Jaws-of-Life to cut your fat ass out of it."

Never a dull moment in the life of a bouncer. Anyway, lets get back to learnin' something. The man on the door has to be a people person. He's one of those kind of guys that everybody likes. He has a nice smile and a friendly manner. My friend Sleazy Larry is like that, the kind of bouncer that everybody likes. He's always laughing and joking with the customers. He's the kind of guy that other bouncers really like to work with.

He's a team player and always in a good mood. Sleazy has a way of making ya laugh when you feel like shit. In the fifteen years I've known Sleazy, I've never heard anybody talk bad about him. I wish I could say the same about myself! Sleazy's got his own style and it works for him.

Now a days, Sleazy is a retired entrepreneur who avoids me because he's scared I'll talk him into working for me! lol. I love ya Sleazy.

On the other hand, there was Jack Shannon. Back in the day, he was Chief of Security at Froggy's Saloon in Daytona Beach, Florida,. I called him Jack Wolf because he reminds me of a timber wolf. The Cree Indians refer to wolves as ghosts of the forest, they have a kind of magic about them. I watched Jack work for ten years. He's the kind of bouncer you can never figure out. He had this thing I call "charisma". (Hell I can't even find it in the dictionary!) Those who knew him liked him and those who didn't like him stay the fuck away from him. Jack was a great cooler.

It's like he was always there even when you didn't see him. When Jack was just standing, he looked like he was not watching, but you can bet your ass he seen it all. He had this ability to make people second guess themselves. Jack worked the door for twenty-five years and had a reputation solid as his skills. Brother Jack Wolf passed on about eight years ago. Fuckin' sad day bro. It always is when a brother passes on. But no matter how good or great a bouncer is, there is that day all old coolers fear. The day its over. The day when you come to 'accept' it is over. There is nothing worse than an old bouncer who can't accept that his bouncing days are over and becomes the joke of the club. No old bouncer wants to see his bag hung on skid-row. Old Doc will clean out his locker with dignity long before that day comes and walk away proud. I never want my boys to carry me or give me a job because they feel they owe me.

That's not how the Legend rolls. When I'm done, the whore will kick me to the curb like the heartless bitch that she is, and I'll take it like a man.

For some bouncers it comes easy because they just got into the trade because they need some extra cash. They walk away from the business and never glance back. But for the bouncer who puts a lifetime of heart and soul into the trade, the end is bitter sweet. It's like I told Brother Davey, Director of WTD (Working The Doors website - England) who interviewed me a few years back.

> *"Being a professional bouncer is like being married to a whore.. It's a thankless job. You are in love with something that can never love you back..and sooner or later she will kill you or leave you wishing she did..."*
>
> Ivan 'Doc' Holiday

A bouncer is very much like a boxer who hits the wall. When every match becomes a struggle. When you eat the pain like candy. When the younger man your fighting is not that fast but your just a second too slow. When wisdom and experience won't carry you into the later rounds.

When the standing eight count is your last.

Let me give you an example of when a great cooler is done.

It was at Froggy's Saloon about ten years back. Jack Wolf was covering for the bar back that called in sick because his pussy was sore. Rockin' Mel was workin the ID door and I was just in for a visit to shoot the shit with Rockin' Mel and Jack. Anyway, this old dude about sixty years old was complaining about his drink being watered down. He started cussing out the bartender Linda. Jack gives Rockin' Mel the signal, Rockin' Mel confronts the old dude. The old dude bows up, Rockin' Mel snatches him up and walks him to the door. No big deal.

This dude looks over at Jack while his is being escorted out and says to Jack *"Your a fuckin faggot!"*

It was at this moment that Jack snapped and totally lost it. Jack ran out from behind the bar and as I moved in to help Rockin' Mel restrain the old dude who was beginning to struggle. Jack Wolf - a bouncer cooler than the Fonz - sucker punches this old bastard right in the mouth while we were holding him! Talk about looking bad on camera!!

I was so surprised. Here I was with my brother Jack Wolf, pushing him back and pinning him against the wall away from the old dude who Rockin' Mel was now dragging out. It was a fuckin mess! Jack's eyes were totally psycho as he stared down the old dude. *"I'll fuckin' kill you!"* Jack yelled over my shoulder. Later that night, when Jack cooled down, he sat on a bar stool looking into his drink. *"I'm done Doc..just can't take the bullshit anymore."* I put a hand on his shoulder *"I hear ya bro."* I replied.

"We all lose our cool now and then Jack." Rockin' Mel said.

Rockin' Mel looked at me and shook his head. He knew it was Jack's last night at the Frog. Rockin' Mel and I loved that old Wolf. May God watch over you Jack 'Wolf' Shannon. One day, God willin' you and I will bounce together at that big biker bar in the sky.

Every bouncer develops his own style. Some guys are good at the door and some are not. A bouncer who is shy or doesn't like to talk is a bad choice to work the door. It doesn't make him a bad bouncer, it just means he's better working inside the club. But if you want to be 100% effective in the trade, a bouncer MUST be able to perform ALL aspects of the trade. He must be as good on the door as he is on the floor. So for this reason I rotate my men so they get equal time at the ID door and in the club to ensure that their skills don't become weak in one area.

If a man is weak in one aspect, I work with him to improve his skills. A bouncer who walks around with a serious look on his face makes people assume he has a bad attitude. Relax and enjoy your work. Son, I can smile, tell you a joke and hit you four times before you get the fuckin' punch line. Its just a metaphor! What I'm saying is you don't want to come across as a hard ass. You want to come across as an easy going guy who can get tough when the going gets rough.

I still remember Curly from when I was just starting out in the business. He was an old Ex-SAS soldier from England. He worked the door for twenty-three years and was tougher than boiled owl shit! I remember it was at the Penalty Box Pub in Edmonton, Alberta, Canada 1982. This black guy came in early one night bragging about winning some Toughman contest. The guy was six foot going about two hundred and twenty pounds. Curly was bald headed, stocky built, five foot eight and weighted about a buck sixty. Curly was leaning against the end of the bar playing with the salt shaker as the black guy approached him. He asked Curly for a job and Curly said he didn't need anyone right now.

The black guy said Curly should hire him because he was better than any of his security. *"I seriously doubt that mate."* said Curly. Curly always backed his men. *"Maybe I'll just kick your ass old man and take your job."*

Curly smiled and said *"Don't let fear and common sense stop you son."*

"Think I'm jivin' fool." the black man said as he stepped

forward. Curly took his foot and slid a bar stool out hitting the black guy in the shins. The black guy tripped up on the stool, threw it to one side and stood up just to catch a hand full of salt in the eyes. When his hands went up to his face, Curly kicked him square in the nuts.

That mother-fucker was wearing his balls for a neck tie! Black dude's eyes rolled back in his head and he was out for the count.

"Ivan" Curly yelled, *"Grab Mikey and drag this piece of garbage outta here!"* He wiped his hands with a bar rag *"Then call the cops and tell them some bum's sleeping in the big dumpster!"* Curly's real name was Nelson. In his Rugby days in jolly old England they called him 'NAILS'.

No fucking wonder. Curly was one tough old bastard!

Now I want to touch on the subject of Motorcycle Gangs.

Real bikers club colors are made up of a vest with the name of the club on the top which is referred to as the *'top rocker'* and the name of their home state on the *'bottom rocker'*. In the center of the vest is the clubs insignia which is referred to as the *'center patch'*.

There are thousands of motorcycle clubs, but then there are the '1% CLUBS'. A 1%ER is a member of the totally zoned out, fucked up, bad-ass, outlaw motorcycle brotherhood. They are sworn by blood to never back down from confrontation, and will fight to the death for their colors. Fuck with one member and you'll have twenty on your neck!

Disrespect a 1%ER or kick him out of your place, he'll come back with his brothers to stomp you to death and burn your shit to the fuckin' ground. They refer to people who are not bikers as 'CITIZENS'.

A biker trying to become a member of a club is called a *PROSPECT or a PROBATE*. Their colors are usually made up of just a bottom rocker with *'Prospect or Probate'* on it. But be careful around these fucker. They are always waiting for a chance to look good in front of the club members and 'make their bones'. 1%ER's carry guns at all times. If not, their ol' ladies are packing the heat for them usually in their Snatch Box (Down the front of their pants).

Let me touch on a subject that a lot of assholes just don't understand. On behalf of my biker brothers I would like to set the record straight. COLORS or a CUT are the vests motorcycle club members wear that have their club insignia on the back. It has nothing to do with T-shirts or tattoos.

Very seldom you'll see a 1%ER with his club colors tattooed on him where he can't cover it. Reason being, should he get kicked out or forced to leave the club he will have to forfeit his colors. This means vest and skin! One time, my step-father used a steel grinder to remove a shoulder tat that resembled a Hells Angels death head off some wannabe biker who was too stupid to take advice and get it blacked out. Not the sharpest tool in the shed. If you see a club T-shirt or tattoo, usually it's some wannabe ass-wipe or a club hang-a-round who buys a *'Support your Local 81"* or *"Support your Local Outlaws"* T-shirt or gets a 'biker tat' to make everybody think that he is a hardcore 1% biker. Now I am not saying that every guy who has a support shirt or a biker tat is a wannabe. I REPEAT..don't be fuckin' stupid and fuck with a 1%ER who is not wearing his colors and just a support T-shirt. A lot of 1% ER's will come into a club undercover to chill and check things out. Sometimes they just want a quiet evening out among the citizens. They will cover tats, have no club insignia on and will blend in. As a rule of thumb, 1% ER's don't show their ass in a club unless they are there on club business and they always show up in numbers. This type of business is usually not good.

1% ER's don't like cameras and if you value your ass, don't take any pictures of their members or their ol'ladies. They won't fuck with you unless you fuck with them first. They will respect bar security as long as they feel that the bouncer is asking, not ordering. Respect is everything with these people. It's best to let the cooler handle delicate situations like these. And NEVER..I mean NEVER ask or tell a 1%ER to take off his colors. EVER! Unless of course you want to have the ever-living dog shit stomped out of you. Not a smooth move Exlax.

It was Sturgis Biker Rally in the Black Hills of South Dakota 2001. I was working at the Broken Spoke Saloon. I had the HA's motorcycle club drop by to 'Talk' with a few members of the IronCross motorcycle club about having Bandit support patches on their colors. Mildly, this means that the HA's did not like the Bandits motorcycle club and 'Anyone' who was 'Associated' with them. The R-rated version, HAMC were at war with the Bandidos MC and any fuckers wearing bandits support shit were gonna get their ass kicked! Anyway, I had this HA prospect come in and sucker punched an IronCross member. Paul a young bouncer who I hired saw what happened and grabbed the prospect. Well the prospect broke loose of Paul's grip and turned to face him holding a 38 snubnose revolver. It was at this time I jumped in between Paul and the prospect with the gun. By now you have probably come to realized I have a real bad habit of doing this. I put my arm around Paul's neck and said,

"You all right son." I soon felt the pressure of the prospect's pistol muzzle against the small of my back. And shit wouldn't you know it..I had no bulletproof vest on! Paul's eyes were big as silver dollars as I could feel his legs starting to get real weak.

At this moment JoB, a friend and HAMC member, came over and told the prospect to get the fuck out.

"*Fuckin' prospect's..always hot and horny to patch in*" JoB shook his head.

"*Sorry about that Doc..probate got off the leash*" JoB grinned.

"*No big deal bro..my boy here didn't know he was one of yours.*" I replied.

The IronCross member who had been hit was already scooped up by his brethren and taken outside. I was holding Paul up as we walked toward the kitchen area. "*I got to piss Doc..*" Paul stated. We stopped by the bathroom and Paul staggered in. I could hear Paul puking his guts out.

Ten minutes later he returned still a little white and shaky. I got one of the boy's to drive him home but I knew he would not be back.

Next day he called me to tell me his Dad needed him to work around the farm. I told him that would be fine and wished him the best.

Bouncing can be dangerous game sometimes but then there are times when the job has its funny moments like I remember back in 1984.

I was working at a club called Beverly Crest Rock Bar. It was early about six pm when I came in. No bouncers were on and there was a young guy in the bar giving the waitress a hard time. The manager, who I might add was a real asshole and a bag licker of the highest order decided to wait for the bouncers.

"*I'll throw him out,*" I told him. I had only started the day before and he didn't know me very well. He started to laugh.

"*You better wait for the bigger bouncers boy,*" he said in his thick Dutch accent. "*I don't want to have to send you to the hospital to have your head removed from your ass.*"

I can still remember his stupid shit eating grin. I was 170lbs at the time and this guy was in town for the open pro football camp. He was about twenty-four years-old, going 6'8" in his cowboy boots.

Tipping the scales at an easy 300lbs.

"I bet ya a hundred bucks I can throw him out," I told Hans.

"It's your funeral, boy," he replied.

"I'm sorry sir, but I have to ask you to leave," I said as I walked up to the table. The guy stood up and at 5'6" tall, my nose was touching against his upper abs. *"Tell me you're not going to try to throw me out?"* he said smiling. Hans was behind the bar and couldn't hear our words over the music.

I poked my finger into his chest hard, and scowled at him.

"You see that faggot over there behind the bar, don't turn your head just look," I told him. He nodded his head. I poked him hard again.

"That son-of-A-Bitch is the manager and the asshole sent me over here to throw you out. He knows I'm the smallest bouncer here and he's lookin' for a reason to fire me so he can hire his brother-in-law on in my place." This time I pointed my finger in his face.

"Mister, I know I can't throw you out because you're bigger than me, but I got four kids and a pregnant wife at home and I need this job."

The big guy winked at me and said, *"I don't want to fuck with you man! I'm outta here."* I followed him to the door and said, *"Thanks man,"* then I yelled, *"and don't come back you fuckin' ape or I'll kick your ass!"* I never got my hundred bucks out of that ignorant bastard but I did watch his wife turn into a first rate fuckin' porno queen before my very eyes on Mikey the DJ's' home video camera.

I thought she was going to fuck that fat little bastard to

death! I'm telling you, for an old broad she had more moves than a two dollar whore! That bitch fell out of a cocksucker tree and hit every limb coming down! Don't take it too hard Hans, she was way too much ass for an old bastard like you anyway. Mikey, for a fat little perverted DJ you had some fuckin' balls. Not only did you fuck the boss's wife but taped it for your pals. I'm sure I speak for all the bouncers reading this book when I say, "Mikey you're one seriously fucked up individual, but we love ya!"

In the words of John The Redman :

"Nice guys finish last . . . bad boys fuck the prom queen!"

7

> *"Keep your friends close and your enemies closer."*
> — Sun-Tzu

Most clubs are usually made up of two or three areas; a main floor, a dance floor and sometimes a billiard area.

Know that these places in each club can be totally different. Some can have an upstairs area, some an outside area, while others can have a basement area.

The three most important factors in bouncing are:
 1. Teamwork
 2. Communication
 3. Position

Teamwork is a given. Basically it is a group of men working together as one unit to accomplish a single task. Goddamn, now you get a chance to see old Doc's intellectual side :)

Bouncers need to work together. It is important to have a good working relationship between you and your fellow bouncers, a close bond of camaraderie. It's like the teams in the military; they develop a respect for each other and the chain of command. From this comes brotherhood and friendship. A bouncer always backs his brother's call. This means if a fellow bouncer wants a person or group of persons removed, the person or persons are to be removed no matter if you feel it is right or wrong. You always side with your brothers. It a kind of unwritten code among bouncers. If you're not happy with the call, wait till after work and discuss it with the cooler.

But in front of the customer's you want to project a positive team image.

Bouncers watch each others backs and take care of one another whether it is in a fight, being a witness on a police report or getting the third degree from the club owner or manager. There is nothing I hate worse than a fuckin' rat or a bag licker! If you have a problem with a fellow bouncer talk to the cooler. He will handle it accordingly. I remember Norm at the Wildwest once told me,

> "There are no homes in this business bro..you can take a bullet for the man and get shit canned the next day."

Communication is most important element of the three. Why because is done by being 'Connected'. With out Connection, bouncers are not a team but a group of individuals working in the same building. The team has to be connected physically by equipment and mentally by being on the same page at the same time. Bouncers communicate by radios, flashlights, lasers or hand signals. I have used hand signals for years. The hearing impaired are an excellent example of the effectiveness of hand signals. I watched them many times sit at a table right beside the loud band speakers and talk to each other through sign language. They can feel the beat through the vibrations in the speakers. Excessive feedback and interference have plagued radios in bars for years, but they are better than no radio communication. You can still hear the radio alarm go off no matter how loud the noise is in a club. Red laser pointers are excellent to get a brothers attention if radio comm is not working or he is not looking at you. You can also point out potential trouble across a packed club.

This is just a tool to help a bouncer and not a fuckin' toy for some immature bouncer to play with. Remember the old saying *"Its all fun and games till someone loses an eye!"*

Never talk personal business on the radio, bar phone or cell phone. They are never secure! Remember all bars have digital security cameras which pick up sounds and can filter voice from music. Bottom line is, you are being monitored in the bar at all times..24-7! Today every peckerhead in the club has a fuckin' cell phone that shoots video. So if your fuckin' up there is a good chance you could be on Utube faster than a cat with a firecracker up it's ass! Professionalism is a bouncer's shield. Keep it with you at all times and stand behind it.

Position is basically being in the right place at the right time. I am known in the bouncing business for my speed. Always first to a problem. The secret of my success is the fact that I am away in the right place at the right time. Most bouncer's avoid crowded areas in a club, but this is usually where trouble starts. I am the opposite and stand in areas where patrons tend to accumulate.

A bouncer needs to know who's watching his back and whether the person or persons are capable of doing just that. I've worked in clubs where the bouncers were not worth a rat's ass and if this is the case then you have to accept that in a fight, you're on your own. Backup is the name of the game in bouncing. Most people who start trouble in a club are not alone. I've worked small bars by myself before and believe me, there's been times when I've thanked a good regular customer for pulling some asshole off my back. As rule of thumb, I don't like or allow patrons to get involved in any bar trouble that does not directly involve them.

But there are those times when a bouncer in a short staff situation may ask a personal friend who is not staff to keep an eye out and watch his back. But now twenty year later, there is no fucking way I am working a door by myself. And here is a prime example :

Bouncer dies after assault in Southampton

A 40-year-old corrections officer from Hampton Bays, who was left in a coma following an assault early Thursday morning at the Southampton Publick House, where he was moonlighting as an ID checker, died on Saturday morning at the Stony Brook University Medical Center. His assailant was arrested minutes later by Southampton Village Police. The death of Andrew P. Reister, a husband and father of two young children, marks the first murder in Southampton Village in 20 years. According to Southampton Village Police. Suffolk County Police homicide detectives have been aiding Village Police in the criminal investigation ever since it became apparent that Mr. Reister would likely die from his injuries. Village Police said that Mr. Reister, a corrections officer for the Suffolk County Sheriff's office, was attacked and choked at the Southampton Publick House shortly after 1 a.m. on Thursday by 25-year-old Anthony Oddone of Farmingville, after telling him to stop dancing on a table. Witnesses told police that Mr. Oddone put Mr. Reister in a choke hold and did not let go even after Mr. Reister had passed out, causing severe brain damage and leaving him in a coma. Several people tried to stop Mr. Oddone, who is 6 feet, 1 inch tall and weighs 175 pounds, according to the New York City Department of Correction.

They performed CPR on Mr. Reister after Mr. Oddone fled the Bowden Square micro-brewery in a taxicab, police said. Southampton Village Police were called to the scene at around 1:10 a.m. Mr. Oddone was apprehended minutes later on North Sea Road, just north of the County Road 39 intersection. Meanwhile, the Southampton Village Volunteer Ambulance took Mr. Reister to Southampton Hospital and he was later transferred to Stony Brook University Medical Center, where he died at 11:08 a.m. on Saturday, according to Suffolk County Police. The Reisters have a 4-year-old daughter, Mary Grace, and 8-year-old son, David, Ms. Dean said. Mr. Reister is also the godfather of her three children, she added. "He is a wonderful, wonderful man ..," Ms. Dean said. "You could only say nice things about him." She then described the attack as a senseless act of violence that will forever change the lives of his family. Though alcohol most likely played a role in the assault, Ms. Dean said, "People have to be responsible for their actions."

Mr. Oddone, an employee of the exclusive Bridge golf club in Noyac and an alumnus of St. Joseph's College in Patchogue, where he studied accounting and business, was arraigned in Southampton Village Justice Court on Thursday afternoon and pleaded not guilty to felony assault charges. However, now that Mr. Reister has died, those criminal charges are expected to be upgraded to murder in the second degree, a felony that carries a potential sentence of 25 years to life.

The Suffolk County District Attorney's Office had no word on Monday afternoon on when a grand jury could indict Mr. Oddone. "Grand jury proceedings are secret by law," spokesman Robert Clifford said.

- By Brendan O'Reilly

IVAN 'DOC' HOLIDAY

This story brings me to tears. I feel so sorry for the Reister Family. Out of respect for Andrew and his family, I feel compelled to tell his story so other's don't make this critical mistake. Andrew had NO backup. NO Team support. This is why I am so against a bouncer working alone.

There is no "I" in 'TEAM' !

When working the floor, it is important that if you are given a specific area or section to work, you remain in that section. Find a good spot and position yourself so you have the best view of the crowd, the waitresses, and the other bouncers in your area. As you scan the crowd take time to visually touch base with the other bouncers in your section. This way, if another bouncer sees trouble and heads for it, you can read his movements and follow him for backup. Stands and perches are excellent for bouncers to get a bird's-eye view of a large crowd, but they should be only about eighteen inches in height and round in shape. The number of security needed in a club depends upon two things: the size of the club and the number of customers per night.

Here's where we run into the lesser of two evils: if one hires twice as many bouncers than needed, unless one has money to burn, money will be wasted on a bunch of bodies in security shirts. They don't make shit, but they don't do shit either! Like I explained previously in the book, you buy ten ink pens on sale for a buck; most of the time only three of them work and the ones that do, don't write worth a shit!

On the other hand, if four good experienced bouncers are hired at ten bucks an hour for a club of six hundred people, you're not going to get the proper security needed.

Yes, some clubs get away with it for a while, but sooner or later the club usually ends up paying for it. Unfortunately, it is usually the bouncers that get the worst of it. Proper ratio for a club or bar is fifty patrons for every bouncer. An outside venue or event seventy-five patrons to every one bouncer. The cooler is never figured into the number of bouncers needed. Reason being, his job is to watch the bouncers to make sure they are doing their job properly and are in their proper positions. For bar owners, the best way to get good security is to hire an experienced cooler who has good solid references from previous employers. Let him help you organize your club's security and hire personnel. He most likely knows a lot of fellow bouncers that are good, and can recommend them. The cooler can also save you money, streamlining your security by hiring pros on a need-only basis. I'm not saying that club managers are not good at hiring security personnel, but sometimes one hires bouncers that have conflicting personalities and this can be a serious problem in the club. For example, a bouncer who's got a beef with the world and feels that everybody is an asshole until they prove him wrong. His attitude is, *'fuck team work, I'm the best and it's every man for himself'*. You can't work with this kind of person in a club that is trying to develop a good security team. I never work with this kind of asshole - period! It's the cooler's ass that is on the line when some dumb-ass manager hires his cousin Bubba as a bouncer because he's family. Give him a god-damn bar back job. Even better, give him your fuckin' job! Do you know how many times I've heard, *"Doc, I know he's a little slow in the thinking department, but look at the size of that sum bitch!"* I need a bouncer, not the fuckin' Grand Champion of some donut eating contest!

There's a big difference between a sumo wrestler and the Pillsbury dough boy! I have worked with some really big men that were overweight but were great bouncers. These men, like sumo wrestlers, are an exception to the rule. The difference?

These men are smart. They can handle their weight and are comfortable with it. They know their limitations and use their weight as an advantage. An old friend Bongo Bob from Edmonton, Alberta, Canada was a prime example. We worked quite a few country clubs together back in the late 1980's. Bongo Bob was about 5'6" tall, 250 lbs. He was one hell of a country dancer and every girl in the place would jump at the chance to dance with him. He was light on his feet for a big man, and he could move faster than a raped ape! Bobby didn't have much education to speak of but that man was one hell of a bouncer!

I can't tell you how many times he went to the parking lot with some pretty boy gym rat calling him fat boy, and proceeded to pound the ever living snot out of the ignorant bastard. Bobby would just smile after and say, *"Weebles wobble, but they don't fall down!"* He was without a doubt one of the best in the business. Be smart when hiring security. It is a very important position in a club. If you feel I am wrong in my judgment, just go a week without bouncers and see.

To run a great club takes teamwork and good communication between management and security. In most clubs the bouncers work as a complete unit. Most of the time an unruly person will get the picture and be ready to listen when confronted by five or six security personnel. Unruly patrons usually feel the bouncer's presence and understand their authority. They know they are in the wrong and one stupid or violent action will bring the bouncers down on them like a pack of wolves.

Bouncers should always try to show up in force when dealing with a hostile situation. There are no heroes in this business, and like I tell my bouncers, *"If you have to roll in the dirt, you didn't make any money that night."* We are not punching bags or people who like to take abuse. We are hired to do a job and get it done in the safest, most efficient way possible. Remember, always watch the cooler's back. When you are having trouble with one person at a table full of people, you always address the group as a whole. If you tell the group that everyone will have to go if they do not settle down, usually the group will get a leash on the trouble maker and make him behave so they don't have to leave.

If you have to talk to a patron sitting with a group, always take him to one side to speak to him. Never make a person look bad or embarrass them in front of others. Most people will respond with anger at being reprimanded in front of friends. When asking someone to leave always be polite and say, *"I'm sorry sir or miss, but management says that you have to leave."* Always use management as leverage. This way you look like a guy just following orders from a higher authority. Thus you can play the good cop, bad cop, scenario if necessary. If this tactic doesn't work use the threat of calling the police and having them trespassed from the property. If a person has to be physically removed, get a bouncer on each arm, one behind to watch the back and one up front to clear the crowd and make room to walk. If the patron is being aggressive take him or her out the nearest exit. Don't drag the mother-fucker the long way through a crowded club kicking and screaming! Not good club PR.

When removing an unconscious or passed out person, wake him and walk him. Be stern but nice. Firm but fair. If he needs a cab, get him one. Don't let a drunk patron drive. Try to talk them into taking a cab. At the exit door inform the doorman that the patron is out for the evening and not to be let back inside. Now over the years I have learned to get the assistance of the drunk patron's friends. If he has buddies, get those idiots to carry his ass home! It ain't rocket science, just find out who he's partying with and hit them with the *"You're responsible for your friend"* card so take his ass home..Period. It works slicker than cat shit on linoleum son!

When removing a person or persons physically, like I said before, always use the nearest exit. You don't bulldog the bastard through the club like a bunch of monkey's trying to fuck a football. CONTROL. You CONFRONT-CONTAIN-CONTROL. Never physically remove a female patron by yourself, always get help. Believe me, nothing can start a fight faster in a bar than a drunk woman with a great ass screaming help in a bar full of hard dicks and heroes. Never get involved in an argument between family members, just tell them to take their problems out of the bar. The way I explain it is real simple: *"I don't give a fuck if you beat your ol' lady or pimp the bitch out.. just don't do it around me or in my bar!"* Metaphorically speaking!

This does not mean that if a person is fearing for their life I would just turn my back on them. We are protectors of those who can't protect themselves. So if a patron fears for their safety, it is your job to protect that person to the best of your ability and/or call local Law Enforcement.

But I will tell you now, domestic disputes in a nightclub are a touchy subject with me and here's why.

I was workin' a club up north in Grand Prairie, Alberta, Canada, called 'The Trumpeter'. I had this scumbag punch his ol'lady in the face. I grabbed the fucker and threw him up against the wall with his arm up his back. His bitch with a bloody nose jumped me from behind and fuckin' near clawed my eyes out! So be real careful when handling family members in a bar. If you think I'm wrong, ask any police officer about handling domestic violence calls! Good time for an ADHD moment..lets hold hands and jump together! ;)

I remember this big Mexican bitch one time at a biker bar I was working at in Monterey, California. This heifer had prison ink on both arms and a pair of jeans with back pockets in two different time zones! I mean whatever cranks your tractor right! Ok. Anyway, Lady Kong got into a pissing contest with a skinny blonde bartender named 'Kitty'. I used to call her 'Fruit loops' cause she reminded me of Toucan Sam, the bird on the cereal box and would never shut up! Well Kitty told Lady Kong to go fuck herself and turned her back to the pissed off rhino on the other side of the bar. Lady Kong reached across and jacked little Miss Kitty over the bar top by her bleach blonde roots! It took four of us to pull that mountain gorilla off of what was left of 'Fruit Loops'. But I do believe the broken nose was a 100% improvement. My buddy got fired for not protecting the bartender and I got fired for punching out the manager for firing my buddy. Now that what I call Brotherhood! The moral of this story is :

Old Doc got three speeds: on, off, and don't push your fuckin' luck! ;)

When handling two fighting groups, stay between the two groups and keep them separated at all times. Always address the aggressor or the most aggressive assholes - first. And NEVER turn your back to a pissed off patron! Unless you want some mother-fucker with a beer bottle or pool cue to hammer you like a hanging curve ball into the cheap seats!

This is where position is so important. It's like a quarterback stepping back into the shotgun. It gives him a chance to view the defense and read the blitz. Plus, if an argument goes from verbal to physical and you're standing a couple of feet back, you can use that distance for momentum to tackle the unruly patron adding leverage and force to your attack. It also gives you room to react if the person should suddenly pull a weapon.

Like I said before, you don't need to crowd the motherfucker. Crowding an angry person is like trying to stick hot butter up a wildcat's ass! He's gonna feel pressured and get even more pissed off. People who are drunk and upset can get a cornered or trapped feeling. Then they start trying to push for room. Be Calm..Be Cool and let the cooler call it. You can now see why I say position is so important. Position is not only important in an area where you have unruly patrons but position is also important to enable you to watch the crowd and your team members. Now if you're busy texting some fuckin' skank or watching the game on the bar TV's..you can stick 'Teamwork, Communication and Position' straight up your ass! You're body's in the club, you're head's in the game on TV or up some bitch's snatch on the cell phone and you are about as useless as a shit flavored lollipop! You're not getting paid to text or watch TV. Your job is to watch your brothers, your staff and your patrons..Period.

This shit makes me madder than a skinhead watchin' Oprah!

Do yourself a favor and lock your cell phone in your car. If an emergency arises have them call the club phone or the manager's cell. Its not worth losing your job over. I have fired four stupid bastard's this year for texting on the job.

Way I would explain it to you is like this:

"See that parking lot...I want to visualize a set of train tracks running down to the street. The tracks are covered with grease and your ass is sitting on them. Fuck up one more time and its Vaya Con Dios Slick!"

A stationary bouncer sees more than a roaming one. Why? A bouncer who is standing on a security stand can put his full attention toward watching the crowd (and not the fuckin' TV's) and does not have to watch where he is walking at the same time. He doesn't have to watch out for a sucker puncher that might be hiding behind the next pillar or dark corner. In a large crowd a roaming bouncer, unless he is over 6ft. tall, has a hard time seeing. As a rule of thumb, I never hire a bouncer under five foot ten inches. Saves me having to deal with possible 'Napoleon' or 'Little Man Syndrome". Last thing I need is some sawed off little juice monkey who wants to beat up any person over five feet-eight inches tall . Face it boys, in this business if you don't use your head, you might as well have two asses! A bouncer assigned an area must stay at his post unless relieved or called to a problem by the cooler. When trouble breaks out get to the problem as quick as possible. This does not give you the right to bull or linebacker your way through the crowd.

I had a young bouncer back in 1990. He was an ex-college football star with nothing to show for it. Just a bunch of trophies and a pain pill habit from a blown out right knee. I felt sorry for the guy and hired him. He saw a person grab another person. He ran through the crowd knocking a table, eight drinks and four people to the floor. One of the four was a girl who broke her ankle in the fall! All this just to find out the two guys were brothers just joking and rough housing around.

No wonder my fuckin' hair is grey!

A bouncer when he is roaming should use all his senses. He needs to let his peripheral vision detect fast motion like running or arms moving. He should keep his ears open for yelling or strange noises. He should watch the patron's faces for signs of anger or fear. Be watching for body language like a shaking fist or pointing finger in anger. Somebody flipping someone off. Also keep your nose to the air for the smell of someone smoking drugs or fire. The cooler roams the room touching base with his bouncers in each assigned area. He is the team captain, the guy that calls the shots. He checks on the bartenders and the other employees to make sure they are OK. This is a big misconception when it comes to the Cooler/Head of Security. It is his job to make sure your doing you're job right! If need be, the cooler fills the spot of a missing or sick bouncer. But overall the cooler is freed up by his team to take care of Cooler business! When addressing people, smile with lips and teeth closed and let your eyes flow softly from person to person. Never staring at any particular person or group of people. Learn to look without anyone knowing that you are looking. I can move past a person who is staring me down, looking at the floor and all the while seeing his every move.

When passing through a large group of people keep your chin down, eyes pealed and jaws clamped shut until you pass through and are in the open. If someone taps you on the shoulder always take two steps ahead before turning to address the person and be ready to duck. Avoid standing in places where someone can get behind you. Always keep your back to the wall or a pillar if possible! Wild Bill Hickok's story concrete's this fact,

On August 2, 1876, James Butler Hickok was playing poker at Nuttal & Mann's Saloon No. 10 in Deadwood, in the Black Hills, Dakota Territory. *(As a matter of fact I bounced at the No.10 Saloon for Lee Ann & her family who have owned the No.10 for over 50 years..now today I hear they have it up for sale..)* Anyway as the story goes, Hickok, as a precaution, always sat with his back to the wall. But this time, the only seat available when he joined his friends at the poker game, was a chair that put his back to a door. Twice he asked another player, Charles Rich, to change seats with him, and on both occasions Rich refused. Wild Bill said fine and sat in the empty chair. A sorry ass mother-fucker named John McCall (better known as "Jack McCall" or "Broken Nose Jack") walked in unnoticed. Jack McCall walked behind Wild Bill and then suddenly drew a pistol and shouted, "Take that!" and fired. The bullet hit Wild Bill in the back of the head, killing him instantly. I have watched the No.10's 'Reenactment' of the Wild Bill Hickok murder one hundred times and I even bought the man who played Wild Bill at the No.10 back in 1999 breakfast over at Kevin Costner's Midnight Star Gambling hall. It was so awesome to be sitting their with dude in his Wild Bill costume! He was a dead ringer for Wild Bill!

His strong southern accent and the way in got into the acting part was just too fuckin' cool!! Swear to God it was like sitting with Wild Bill in the flesh! Those were the days bro. Anyway, let continue on.

Never let your guard down and keep your back to the wall whenever possible. I wouldn't tell you this shit if it wasn't important.

Old Doc knows all about getting bushwhacked by a coward in a Bar.

It was the at the Long Riders country and western bar in Calgary 1991. I had a sucker puncher step from behind a pillar and hit me with a taped up roll of pennies in my face fracturing my jaw. I caught the dance floor hand rail and didn't go down. When he saw this, he panicked threw down the weapon and made a run for the exit. My brother Marlboro and two more bouncers tackled him before he could get out. Talk about being up to your ass in alligators! My brother's were on him like wild dogs on a three legged cat. Hell the manager had to drive me to the emergency room because the sucker puncher needed the ambulance!

When a bouncer goes to the bathroom to check it out he makes sure to have a team member keep an eye out for him. If you have to piss never use the stand up urinals, ALWAYS use the toilet and make sure to close the door and lock it behind you. I saw a guy get kicked in the balls from behind while taking a piss and it wasn't a pretty sight. If someone wants to fuck up a bouncer that's a goddamn good way to do it! I'm five foot six inches tall, and two hundred and twenty-five pounds. I'm kind of built like a gorilla, short legs, thick chest, and long arms. But I can move through a crowd and never hit a person. My boss says I move though a crowd like a ghost.

I told him, a soldier has to be able to traverse thick jungle, read the terrain, and become one with it. He must be able to watch the ground for traps and the bush for enemy. Sometimes the jungle canopy is so thick that the sunlight cannot penetrate through it, so you have a lot of shadows and dark area's. To top it all off, a steady down pour of rain that can last for days. You lose it in there brother, and you're in a world of hurt!

When passing by a person where there is no room, put your hands on their hips or shoulders and steady them as you slide by. Make sure you identify yourself as security. People don't usually mind you brushing against them or putting your hands on them as long as it is done in a friendly and professional manner. Always say, *"Excuse me sir or Miss"* and *"Thank you"* after you pass by if possible. Good time for a story.

I was working at the Broken Spoke Saloon for Daytona Bikeweek and it was eight am. Our night watchman called in sick so I had to work that night and pull over night security. So needless to say old Doc was tired and ready to go home to catch some *ZZZZ*. I noticed two guys walking up toward me. An older man, tall skinny wearing a ten gallon cowboy hat and a short fat bearded man in a camo baseball hat. Ok lets see if I can give you a better visual of these two clowns. The taller old dude looked like Woody the cowboy doll from the Disney movie TOY STORY with an seventy year old Sam Elliot head on it! Yes, I probably would screw your drunk girlfriend and lie to you about it..but this is the God's truth! The short fat-man was an identical twin for John William Young aka 'Tinker' from the movie ROADHOUSE. OK, you got the picture. So the two strangers come walking up to me.

"*Howdy partner..my name is 'Big T'.*" the taller man stated.

'*Okey dokey*' thought to myself. I smiled and pointed at his Xtra-large belt buckle with the Texas Star on it. "*Some say that's a head stone for a dead prick*" I blurted out. "*Just fuckin' with ya Tex..*" I recanted, struggling hard not to burst out in hysterical laughter. The tall man looked at me totally confused. I quickly pointed at short fat man standing beside him.

"*who's this...Little T*" I grinned. "*Hell no...that's mikey*" the tall man replied.

"*Anyway*" Big T continued, "*We're the COOLERS your manager Joe Wyse hired..*" Big T bowed up and stuck his thumbs in his belt.

"COOLERS?" I repeated. " *Experts son..Pros!*".

"*Right...OK..*" I smirked. "*What do you do round here partner..*" Big T asked me. "*I am hired to remove unruly patrons from places that serve alcoholic...*" I stated in a sarcastic tone.

"*Ahhh..bar back..aye*" Big T replied. "*Close enough partner..*" I smirked. "*Do me a favor slim..*" I said as I turn to leave. " *If you see Joe Wyse, tell him Doc said 'YOUR FUCKIN' KILLIN ME'!*"

Well Big T and Mikey never got hired and peckerhead Joe

Wyse avoided me for most of the night. Just another day at the OK Corral.

In most clubs dance floors are a real hot spot for trouble. People are up close and personal. Nowadays we have the hip-hop scene. Dudes dressed like rodeo clowns with their pants saggin' and asses hanging out. The bitches are into ass worship! Big butt's wearing shit so tight you couldn't drive a toothpick up their ass with a sledgehammer. Pimpin' their junk on the dance floor like a fuckin' paint shaker at Home Depot!

That idiot Eminem puts it like this : '*There she goes shaking that ass on the floor , Bumpin and grindin that pole.. The way she's grindin' that pole I think I'm losing control* 'Well..I think you're a dumbass!

Talk about fuckin' bouncer distraction! So add to the pot a bunch of stiff dick's lookin' for a freestanding lap dance and you got problems. One huge issue is when I get some totally wasted skank bent over like a dog in a breeding stand, getting her ass grinded by some dickhead. She then gets all pissed off when she comes to the realization that the hard-on she's been grinding for the last ten minutes is not her boyfriend's!

Big time fuckin' drama unfolds on dance floors. When setting up the bouncer's stands, put them on both sides of the stage so they can see one hundred and eighty degrees, facing the dance floor. Don't put them too close to the stage lights, smoke machine or the dance floor lasers. It will blind the bouncers and make it impossible to supervise the people on the dance floor. Also when standing on the stands it's good to maintain a bouncer's basic hands-in-front stance. Protect those Family Jewels! Regulars to a local bar are usually easy to deal with if you handle them in a professional manner. Now a big problem I see is when bouncers start getting to know the regulars. You need to set the boundaries of what is considered professional conduct-ASAP. Bottom-line: don't play grab ass with your customers! Patrons are like little kids, they don't know when enough is enough. If you act unprofessional, you will be treated unprofessional. Don't horseplay with the patrons. Be professional when at work and conduct yourself in a professional manner at all times.

The worst thing you can do to a regular is to bar him from the premises for a certain amount of time, especially if it's the best place in town and all his friends go there. Just the threat of barring him is usually enough to detect a regular from any further bad behavior. Never let a waitress sling drinks after last call. This is some greedy bitch who gets an extra tray full of drinks and dumps it off on a couple of poor bastards.

They end up buying a tray full of booze only to have the bouncer take it because it's three a.m. They get pissed off and the bouncer has to deal with the shit!

In famous words of Doc Holiday:

"The perfect patron is one who comes in the bar, gets drunker than three barrels of shit, turns into an asshole and throws himself out!"

I would have to say that the worst area to have trouble in would be the billiard area. Think of the number of things that can be used as a weapon!

When drinking and gambling are mixed, you're going to have problems. Any kind of gambling is against the law in a bar unless the bar has a license for it, but in clubs and bars it has gone on for years. We usually just ignore it unless it gets out of hand. I've had more than a couple of pool cues busted over my back through the years. Matter of fact, I'm headed out to Los Angeles, California with my son Caine to a bar called

'The Roadkill Bar & Grill' for my new Reality TV show. Last week a biker snapped a cue off on the side of a pool table and stabbed a guy in the guts with it! My kind of place, all warm and fuzzy like.

You also get the guys who like to shoot pool and have their own breakdown cues. The cues make great weapons later on after they leave the billiard area and sit in the bar area. When working a billiard area remember one important thing, billiard balls used as long range projectiles work better than a pool cue. You get hit by a fifty mph billiard ball brother, you'll drop the cue! I once had a guy in a Redneck bar out in Phoenix pull a buck knife on a cowboy in the billiard area. He forced him up against the wall. I picked the 8-ball up off the table and fired it a him, hitting him in the back. He went down like a ton of bricks, and ended up with three cracked ribs. The billiard area is a dangerous area. Be very careful when working this section.

I worked at a place called Rock City, in Edmonton Alberta, Canada back in 1985 which shared the same building with a kick boxing club. One night three young black guys came in and started trouble in the billiard area. When I tried to talk to one of them he swung at me. I slipped the punch and stepped back as he jumped up and kicked me, propelling me over the billiard table. When he didn't see me rise from behind the table he ran around it to finish me off. When he came around the corner of the table I was crouched down and smashed him across the knees with a mechanical bridge. Dropped this chickenhead like a bad habit!!

The mechanical bridge for you who are not familiar with billiard terms, is a pool cue with a steel 'W' shaped end which is used to help a players make shots that are too far to reach. They are heavy in weight and are always stored under the tables, as this stupid bastard found out the hard way! In the paper next day I read that the visiting Jamaican Taekwondo Champion had to cancel his up coming exhibition match with the Canadian champion. He had suffered a broken knee in a night club downtown, but they didn't give any other information. The champ's training camp people came to see me next day. I told them that the bar was not a training room for their boys to get a little exercise and use my brothers for punching bags. These suits were running their mouths like a boarding house toilet! I told them to keep their shit on a leash and out of my bar and to tell Mr. Dreadlocks he's lucky I didn't ram that pool cue up his black ass!

I guess you could say he got some bad JuJu from a pool cue, Mon!

Bathrooms should be checked regularly because people use them for smoking drugs and making their drug deals. I was working at a bar with a bouncer named Karen MacDonald back in 1988 at a place called the Cadillac Ranch. Karen was a blackbelt Taekwondo instructor. One Saturday night Bongo Bob and I were at the door watching the dance floor. As the country dancers came around the far corner, Bongo and I could only see the dancers' heads and shoulders then they would disappear from sight. After the third couple vanished from sight I took a walk over to see what the hell was going on. Here was this guy, drunker than three barrels of shit, leaning on the dance floor railing watching the dancers with his dick hanging out pissing a steady stream across the floor. No one had noticed! Six people had slipped and fallen in the piss. Karen came running over with Bob.

"*Throw him out, Karen,*" I said. She looked at the guy with his weasel hanging out and a shit-eating grin on his face.

"*I am not going to touch that disgusting son of a bitch!*" she replied.

"*But you're the bouncer and it's your job,*" I said, winking at Bongo Bob.

"*Fuck you and the horse you rode into town on*" she fired back.

Bobby and I escorted our fireman and his four inch hose to the door. On the way back in I grabbed a book of matches from the counter and handed them to Karen.

"*The guy gave me his phone number to give to you. I think he likes you, Grasshopper.*"

"*You are such an asshole.*" She smiled and punched me in the arm.

I miss you Karen. You were one of the good ones.

If you are ever in a situation in a club that you feel you cannot handle in a professional manner, let the other bouncers handle it and walk away. Go to the bathroom, splash some cold water on your face and take a minute to chill out. There have been times in my career when a patron just gets under my fuckin' skin, pushing all the right buttons and all I want to do is wipe my ass with his face! At these times I am smart enough to have fellow bouncers takeover. I just walk away, let the brothers take care of it and say the three magic words to myself that every bouncer needs to know, they are, "*Let it go*". Then I take five and go get a cup of shitty bar coffee that's too thick to drink and too thin to plow!

Well, I guess this is the end of my book.

I believe, as one bouncer to another, the best way to say goodbye is over a hot cup of shitty bar coffee and a slice of cold pizza. Next to Tylenol and Tiger Balm, it's the breakfast of champions for any old bastard crazy enough to still be workin' the door after all these years.

Next March 8th it will 30 years I've been a bouncer...if I live to see it!

I hope you enjoyed my book. I hope you learned something from it, so that all the blood my brothers and I have shed over the years was not in vain. You know, it's really sad when I talk to a younger bouncer and he cops an attitude with me. I try to talk to him like a man and comes off like a punk giving me this 'ya right Pops' attitude. My grandfather told me on the day I went into the Army,

> "A person who thinks he knows it all.. is a person who never learned anything."

Rockin' Mel and his son Red Dog Melvin were with me at the Big Smoke cigar shop last week. Melvin asked me,
"When you gonna retire from bouncing Doc?"
"You'll probably read about it in the Obituary column.." I replied and winked at Rockin' Mel.

I remember sitting one night with an old Vietnam vet who was workin' the door in a shit hole, in some one-horse town in the middle of butt-fuck-nowhere. It was snowing outside and the north wind was blowing cold as a whore's heart. He sat across from me and stared at the coffee cup he held in his hands. I couldn't help but notice all the scars he had. The silver wedding band on his finger was as tarnished as the dog tags that hung around his neck. I wondered how many brothers he'd lost in Vietnam and how many demons came back to haunt him in that coffee cup each night? He spoke without lifting his eyes, but I could feel them on me.

"I've got my scars" he said, lifting the cup to his lips. "Some I got in Nam but most I got workin' in bars." I watched him as he ran his thumb over the silver band. "But I'll tell you Doc it's the ones you can't see that hurt the most." He took a sip of his coffee, and stared out the window at the snow falling in the darkness.

I raised my coffee cup to my lips and said, "Amen soldier .. Amen".

The Ten Commandments of Bouncing

1. No one ever wins a fight.
2. Know yourself.
3. Expect the unexpected.
4. Never underestimate anyone.
5. Never lose control.
6. Respect everyone.
7. Have compassion and understanding for others.
8. Never speak ill of others.
9. Never touch alcohol or drugs when working.
10. Never take things personal.. remember it's just a job.

About the Author

Ivan Holiday Arsenault was born in New Brunswick, Canada. Received an honorable discharge from the Canadian Armed Forces in 1980. In 1981 joined Burns Security and worked as personal security to the French Ambassador to Canada in Edmonton, Alberta Canada. In 1982 Ivan worked his first bouncing job at the Forum Inn in Edmonton, Alberta. At 52 years old, Ivan "Doc" Holiday has worked a total of 55 nightclubs and bars over a period of 28 years. He is recognized worldwide as a leading authority in the field of nightclub security. Ivan is the author of the book "The Bouncer's Bible – The Art and Science of working the door", "The Cooler's Grimiore -The Comprehensive Instructional Guide to Nightclub & Bar Security" and "Sun Tzu & The Art of Bouncing".

In 1999 he produced the World's First and only Nightclub Security Instructional Video under the Bouncer's Bible DVD title. Ivan is the founder and president of BouncerGear Inc Nightclub & Bar Security Academy. He is a Registered

Bodyguard with SEAL Bodyguard International - Canadian Government file # TN57496. Former Alumni Member of Blackwater Worldwide- Member # F0B0502.

In 2008 Ivan deployed to IRAQ as a Honeywell Defense Contractor to train US Army soldiers in a new Stryker Recovery System.

Ivan is a Canadian autodidact and MENSA America member with a WAIS-III I.Q. score of 144.

Links

http://outskirtspress.com/webpage.php?ISBN=9781432726416
My book the Cooler's Grimiore

http://www.youtube.com/watch?v=OqigrPnoV4o
My Reality TV Trailer

http://www.youtube.com/watch?v=xCr6i72L77k&feature=related
Doc interview

http://www.youtube.com/watch?v=gxJrTJy0Hfw
Doc UKTour

http://www.bouncergearcorp.com

http://www.roadhousereality.com

http://www.riversidecafe.com

http://guard.dk/karriere/guard-group-academy

http://www.get-licensed.co.uk

http://www.blackhawksecurity.ro

http://www.workingthedoors.co.uk

http://bounceronline.proboards.com

http://www.closeprotectionworld.co.uk

http://en.wikipedia.org/wiki/Bouncer_%28doorman%29